Neh 8:10

SPIRITUAL WARFARE FOR CATHOLICS

Light of Christ

Prayer Group

534-2806

Spiritual Warfare
for Catholics

Father Jeffrey J. Steffon

CHARIS

Servant Publications
Ann Arbor, Michigan

Scripture quoted by permission. All quotations unless otherwise indicated are from *The Holy Bible: New International Version.* Copyright (c) 1973, 1978, 1983 International Bible Society. Used by permission of Zondervan Publishing House. All rights reserved.

Published by Servant Publications
P.O. Box 8617
Ann Arbor, Michigan 48107

The names and characterizations in this book are drawn from the author's case studies or his personal experience and are rendered pseudonymously and as fictional composites. Any similarity between the names and characterizations of these individuals and real people is unintended and purely coincidental.

Cover design by Eric Walljasper

93 94 95 96 97 10 9 8 7 6 5 4 3 2 1

Printed in the United States of America
ISBN 0-89283-847-7

Library of Congress Cataloging-in-Publication Data

Steffon, Jeffrey J., 1954-
    Spiritual warfare for Catholics / Jeffrey J. Steffon.
        p.   cm.
    Includes bibliographical references.
    ISBN 0-89283-847-7
    1. Spiritual warfare.   2. Demonology–Catholic Church.   3. Catholic Church–Doctrines.   4. Catholics–Religious life.   I. Title.
BT981.S735 1994
235'.4–dc20
                                                                    94-18166
                                                                    CIP

For all bishops and priests
who struggle in the Lord's vineyard,
may God's blessings be upon
their lives and ministries.

Contents

Acknowledgments

I thank those who have supported me throughout the writing of this book, who are too numerous to mention. I thank my priest support group for their prayers. I thank Rachel Orega-Gonzales for proofreading the text. And I thank the parishioners of Precious Blood Parish for their prayers.

Introduction

*

Dave was a good Christian man. He came to church regularly and had a good prayer life. He was a faithful husband and a good father, teaching his children good moral values. Dave tried to follow God's commands with all his heart and was a model parishioner.

But Dave had a problem that he could not get rid of. He was drawn to pornography. Occasionally, he would put himself in harm's way. But the temptations to buy a pornographic magazine or video would usually appear suddenly in his mind. It was as if they came from out of the blue. Sometimes he was able to resist these temptations, but other times he gave in to them.

Whenever he succumbed to these temptations, Dave felt terrible. He would think, "How could I have done this? I must be a horrible person." He knew it was wrong, but he felt so oppressed with the thoughts that he could not help himself. His life was becoming a battleground, and he was starting to give in to despair. The more he gave in to these thoughts, the more depressed he became.

Maybe you have experienced something similar. Have you

ever had temptations that seem to come out of the blue? Have you been oppressed with sinful thoughts and inclinations? Have you felt that no matter how hard you tried, you just could not resist the sin? Do you ask, "How could I have done this?"

In Dave's situation and in ours, it is important to know the source of the temptations. Some of it may well be normal human inclinations. God made us male and female, and there is a natural attraction between the sexes. If we did not have a desire for the opposite sex, we would not marry and have children. Without children the human race would be extinct. So the sexual drive is not evil. It was made by God and when expressed in love in a valid marriage, it is holy and blessed. But when sex is used in improper ways, it becomes sinful.

There may well have been a number of reasons for Dave's recurring problem with pornography. Maybe Dave had emotional problems that he needed to resolve. The thoughts of pornography and illicit sex could stem from abuse in his childhood. It could also derive from poor emotional development. Or maybe he had lustful thoughts when he stopped at a newsstand and looked at the covers of pornographic magazines, instead of just passing by.

But there could be another source of these temptations. Since they usually came from "out of nowhere" and were strong and insistent, they could have come from an outside source—Satan. Only by using proper discernment would it be possible to know the source or sources of his temptations.

The same is true in our lives. We experience temptations to sin. What is the source of our sinful inclinations? And once we know the source, how do we deal with it?

A SPIRITUAL WORLD

The first step in this process is to realize that we are living in a multidimensional world. We are physical beings—we have a body and are finite. We also have a mind and emotions. And we have a spiritual part as well. We must admit that we are living in not only a physical universe, but also a spiritual world. It is only when we acknowledge the reality of the spiritual world that it is possible to discern properly the root causes of difficulties in our lives.

The Book of Revelation describes a spiritual battle:

And there was war in heaven. Michael and his angels fought against the dragon, and the dragon and his angels fought back. But he was not strong enough, and they lost their place in heaven. The great dragon was hurled down—that ancient serpent called the devil, or Satan, who leads the whole world astray. He was hurled to the earth, and his angels with him.

Then I heard a loud voice in heaven say: "Now have come the salvation and the power and the kingdom of our God, and the authority of his Christ. For the accuser of our brothers, who accuses them before our God day and night, has been hurled down. They overcame him by the blood of the Lamb and by the word of their testimony; they did not love their lives so much as to shrink from death. Therefore rejoice, you heavens and you who dwell in them! But woe to the earth and the sea, because the devil has gone down to you! He is filled with fury, because he knows that his time is short." **Revelation 12:7-12**

The Devil is not a symbol or a legend. He is very real. Originally he was an angel of God, but through his own pride he became corrupt. He refused to be obedient to the will of God, and because of his rebellion he and his followers were cast out of heaven. In his fury he now tries to destroy those who seek to follow God. Satan, the accuser, tries to tempt us and destroy us. He does his best to thwart the plan of God. God's plan is that we know him, love him, serve him, and live with him forever in heaven. Satan wishes to destroy this plan. He tried to damn the whole human race in the Garden of Eden.

In Genesis 3:1-21, Satan, disguised as a serpent, set about on his evil plan. He wished to corrupt the crown of God's creation, Adam and Eve, our ancestors. Satan, the angel who rebelled against God, wanted to lead them into rebellion as well, to thwart the wonderful plan of God.

So he tempted Eve by tricking her, convincing her to doubt God's goodness. He implied that God was strict, stingy, and selfish, reserving the knowledge of good and evil for himself alone. Eve, in her weakness, fell into his trap. She believed the words of the great liar. She forgot all that God had given her and desired the one thing that God had set off limits—the fruit of the tree of good and evil. Then she shared her disobedience with Adam, and he also rebelled and ate of the forbidden fruit. Instead of obeying God's clear command, he also accepted Satan's lies.

Notice how Satan worked. He used a sincere motive to tempt Eve—"you will be like God." It is not wrong to want to be like God. Our goal is to grow in being more like him each day. But Satan tricked Eve into thinking that she could become like God through disobedience, defying God's authority as Satan himself had in the heavenly battle recounted in Revelation.

Satan also tried to make sin look good and desirable. It would be advantageous to have knowledge of good and evil, he told Eve. With his craftiness he deceived our first parents. After their sin, they were ashamed and experienced the first pangs of human guilt for sin. They tried to hide from God in their shame. And thus we see the same patterns of sin repeated in our own lives—pride and deception followed by guilt and shame. Such are the effects of original sin which have been passed on by our first parents. Of course, pride and deception are only two prominent sinful tendencies among many that we must battle in our fallen state.

Because of their sin, Adam and Eve lost the special gifts that they had received, but they did not lose their most precious gift because God promised to send a Redeemer. Even though they had disobeyed God, he did not abandon them. In his great love for them God made them garments, wishing to protect them from harm. What love God had for our first ancestors, and what tremendous love God has for us! When we disobey God, like Adam and Eve, he will still forgive us if we but turn to him. He sent his only Son, Jesus, to free us from our sins. Through Jesus we have redemption. It seemed that all was lost, but in the Father's plan, we are made new through the Blood of Jesus Christ. God is so loving and merciful!

But Satan, on the other hand, is full of hatred. His goal is to destroy us, the followers of God. He tries to lure us away from God's ways with empty promises, just like he tempted Adam and Eve with the promise that they could be like God by disobeying him.

He promises power and money, but he cannot deliver on his promises. Absolute power and greed lead to corruption and that is all Satan can offer—corruption, lust, greed, and every vice known to the world. His promises and allurements will never bring peace. They will only lead us to eternal death. We are truly in a battle—a spiritual battle for the salvation of our souls.

We receive the pledge of salvation from Jesus, who through his precious Blood has conquered Satan. We are victorious in him, but we do not always feel victorious. That is because Satan, though he is defeated, still wages guerilla warfare upon the followers of Jesus.

But we are not alone. We have a special group of believers

standing ready to help us. All we have to do is to call upon them for assistance. For instance, the angels are the messengers of God who are many times sent to protect and guide us. Each of us has been given a guardian angel to help us grow in holiness and protect us from evil. The saints as well stand before the throne of God, waiting to assist us with prayers.

Among the saints, Mary, the mother of Jesus, is a very important intercessor for us. Jesus, as he was dying on the cross, said to his mother, "Dear woman, here is your son," and to the disciple, "Here is your mother" (Jn 19:26-27). The disciple at the cross is our representative. Jesus, in these words, established a special relationship between Mary, his mother, and all Christians that the disciple represents. Mary is not just another holy woman. Jesus' intent in this action is to give Mary a special place in the heart of all his followers.

Just as Mary loved and cared for her child Jesus, so Mary also has a love for us, her spiritual children. Just as a mother wants the best for her child, so Mary desires the best for us. And the best thing for us is union with Jesus Christ. Mary, the mother of Jesus, wishes to unite us to the heart of her Son. With the saving Blood of our Redeemer and the assistance of Mary, the saints, and the angels, it is possible to ward off the attacks of Satan and his demonic spirits.

THE BATTLEGROUND

Our lives are the battleground of this spiritual warfare. Satan tries to aggravate existing difficulties that we have because "the devil prowls around like a roaring lion looking for someone to devour" (1 Pt 5:8). He directly and indirectly attacks our weaknesses, for his sole purpose is to destroy God's life within us. He attacks our minds and emotions. He tries to undermine our conscience and lead us into sin. He aggravates the inner pain we experience.

If he cannot attack us in our minds and emotions, he executes a secondary plan. He attacks us through the world and our own fleshly and sinful desires. He tries to contaminate us spiritually through places that are infested with his presence or through people who are following his ways. Remember, every person we meet is not necessarily sent to us by God. Sometimes Satan tries to deceive us through his agents. I do not mean to say that these people are evil (though some of them may be, at least in part), but some people can be manipulated by Satan to adversely affect our spiritual lives. He also aggravates our own sinful tendencies and desires—be they a tendency toward laziness and procrastination or deception and dishonesty, for example.

Further, he tries to lure us into bondage to him through the occult. When we become involved in any part of the occult, we give part of our lives to Satan. Practicing the occult is asking him for power or knowledge. We may receive what we need, but the price we pay for his help is our eternal salvation.

We truly are besieged by this adversary, but not all problems are directly from him. The root causes of our difficulties may well be multidimensional, as we saw in the case of Dave and pornography. There can be spiritual causes which stem from a weak spiritual life. God has a remedy for these kinds of problems: forgiveness and prayer.

Psychological and emotional problems can also affect our choices. I believe that the solution to these sorts of problems is usually counseling and inner-healing prayer. We may also need to avoid occasions of sin.

Further, there can be circumstantial or physiological causes to our difficulties, or we may suffer from a chemical imbalance in the brain.

We need proper discernment to know the root causes of our problems. And we must remember—Satan wishes to aggravate an existing agony. Therefore, we must be aware of his deceptions.

OUR WEAPONS IN THE BATTLE

As we have seen, God has not left us alone in this battle. He has given us the power of the holy name of Jesus to renounce involvement in the occult and break any demonic oppression we may be experiencing for whatever reason. Wherever the name of Jesus is pronounced by a believer, Satan shudders in fear. God has given us special protection in his holy armor (Eph 6:12-18). We have heavenly intercessors in Mary and the saints, waiting to assist us with their prayers, and spiritual helpers and protectors in the angels, especially our own guardian angel.

In addition to the name of Jesus and a heavenly army of helpers, God has given us the sacraments—special graces to protect us from evil and draw us into his loving heart. Through the sacraments, particularly Holy Communion, we unite ourselves with Jesus and he brings us to the throne of our Father. Further, whenever we need forgiveness from sin, we can approach the Father's throne of grace through Jesus and experience the joy of reconciliation by going to confession. We also have the protection of sacramentals, such as holy water and crucifixes, to keep the Evil One away from our homes and possessions.

We have every weapon necessary to defeat the Evil One. We simply need to use them with the proper dispositions. But even then we may still become discouraged. We may be tempted to despair. We cannot allow ourselves to fall into this trap. We are a people of hope! We hope in the Lord because he delivers us from sin. We hope in the promises of God—he will never abandon us in our need. After all, God has entered into a sacred covenant with us. Satan cannot destroy us as long as we hope in the Lord our God.

OVERVIEW OF THIS BOOK

My goal in writing this book is to help us Catholics know and use the weapons in our spiritual arsenal to protect us from the power of Satan. In the first part of this book I discuss the spiritual world. In the first two chapters, I talk about the importance of faith and the reality of Satan, demonstrating this diabolical reality through the Scriptures and through Catholic tradition. Then I explain the power that we possess in the Blood of Jesus. Jesus has redeemed us and given us power over the Evil One. I also introduce Mary, the angels, and the saints as our heavenly helpers.

In the second part I describe the battleground of spiritual warfare and how Satan attacks us, both internally and externally. Satan wishes to aggravate existing problems in our lives and uses the flesh and world to ensnare us. Chapter eight then describes how the resulting demonic oppression typically works. We must learn how to use the gift of discernment to know if there is a demonic oppression in our lives.

Chapter nine describes the weapons that we have at our disposal for this warfare and explains in more detail how to use them. We have so many gifts from God. We possess the power of the name of Jesus and the armor of God. We have special prayers to help us be free of the occult and grow in holiness. We can ask Mary and the saints to intercede for us. God has given us guardian angels to instruct us in his ways. We have the special graces of the sacraments, especially Holy Communion and the sacrament of reconciliation, to empower us to live a life following the will of our Father. And we have the sacramentals to protect us from demonic harassment. We have everything that we need to be victorious against Satan and the demonic spirits.

We must remember who we are—adopted sons and daughters of God! Jesus has won the victory for us and he will never leave us. No power, whether it be earthly or unearthly, can separate us from his love. Blessed be the holy name of Jesus through whom we share in victory over the Evil One.

PRAYER TO SAINT MICHAEL

Saint Michael, The Archangel,
defend us in the battle.
Be our protection against the wickedness
and snares of the Devil.
May God rebuke him, we humbly pray,
and do thou, O Prince of the Heavenly Host,
by the power of God, thrust into hell
Satan and all evil spirits
who wander through the world
for the ruin of souls.
Amen.

PART ONE:

The Spiritual World

ONE

Faith

Faith is being sure of what we hope for and certain of what we do not see (Heb 11:1). Two words describe faith: sure and certain. The beginning point of faith is believing in God. The end point is believing in God's promises. When we believe that God will fulfill his promises, though we don't see those promises materializing, we demonstrate true faith. Part of faith is an expectancy. We expect that God will be true to his word.

But there is an underlying presupposition to faith—belief in God. We place faith in a person, not a thing. First we must ask ourselves: Who is God? What type of a God do I believe in? Do I believe in a personal God or an impersonal God? Do I believe in the God that is revealed in the Bible, or do I have another reference point for my belief in God? This is key. If I believe in the God of the Bible, do I accept other revelation contained in the Bible? This faith is the foundation for our lives and our system of beliefs.

It is only from this starting point, belief in God—a supreme being, the Creator of the universe—that we can begin to understand the nature of the spiritual world. If I do not believe in God, then a discussion of the spiritual world and the spiritual battle makes no sense. But if I do believe in God, then I am open to explore the spiritual world.

Is there really a God? How can I be sure? Is it simply that I believe, that I have faith in an all-powerful being who created the heavens, the earth, and all that they contain? Or did this world simply begin by the power of two atoms whirling in space and then suddenly colliding together? How did things come to be? How did this world, our solar system, and the universe come into being? How did life begin?

Philosophers throughout the ages have been asking these questions. Even today there is a debate about the universe's origins. Did it occur through evolution or an act of creation? Or could it be a combination of both? Did the world just happen? Are we humans solely the product of mutations that have come through evolution? Or are we products of divine intervention?

At St. John's Seminary, I studied the history of philosophy with my fellow seminarians. In philosophy a person tries to explain their experiences. From their experiences, they make a statement about the world or how people receive knowledge from the world. In our courses we studied the early philosophers (Socrates, Plato, and Aristotle), as well as the great Catholic medieval philosophers (St. Augustine, St. Bonaventure, and St. Thomas Aquinas). We also studied the modern philosophical movements of existentialism, pragmatism, and phenomenology. Each philosopher we studied had a theory about the existence of the world.

The Catholic philosophers tried to prove the existence of God. In his writings, St. Thomas Aquinas presented arguments for belief in God. But before one accepts all of St. Thomas' arguments or proofs for the existence of God, one must realize that St. Thomas was primarily a theologian.

In other words, St. Thomas first believed in God, then he tried to explain reasons why he believed in God. St. Thomas was primarily a person of faith. His arguments for God helped people of faith to understand that faith in God is reasonable. He did not prove the existence of God. Other philosophers like Kant, Nietzsche, and Marx have denied the existence of God and developed arguments to support their positions.

Who is correct? And how was this world created? One answer to this question is to believe that the universe always existed and that it always will. That is something we cannot prove. Another possible answer is to believe that there was a tremendous burst of energy when two atomic particles collided. That burst of energy created the universe. But from where did the two atomic particles come? Another solution to this question is that there is a being who is eternal; this being created the universe. We call this being God.

I believe that God created the universe. God has given me the gift of faith; everything in the spiritual life begins with this faith. Either I believe in God or I do not believe in God. This belief in God is a gift. God's existence cannot be proved (that is, reasoned to), but belief in God is reasonable. God, in his generosity, has revealed himself to those who believe in him.

My belief in God is going to affect my life in the world. Why do I choose to live the way that I do? What is right and what is wrong? Is there a code of morality by which I am called to live? Is there a life after death, eternal reward or eternal punishment? All the answers to these questions come from our faith perspective. It is impossible to live without a code of morality or beliefs. My beliefs will affect every decision that I make. Even if I do not believe in God, I still live by some ethics, whether they be based in another religion or a humanistic belief system.

Since I believe that the Bible is the revealed Word of God, I find my code of morality in God's Word and his promises. And I also find information about a spiritual world in the Bible. This material world is not the only world that we live in. We are part of another reality. It is only when we acknowledge the reality of the spiritual world that it is possible to discern properly the reasons behind our actions.

Then, what is this spiritual world? What is contained in it? According to the Bible, the spiritual world consists of God, who is Father, Son, and Holy Spirit; the angels (God's special ministers to help us in our lives); the saints (those who have died and are in heaven interceding for us on earth before God's throne—including preeminently Mary, the mother of Jesus); and demonic spirits.

Saint Paul tells us to "put on the full armor of God so that you can take your stand against the devil's schemes. For our struggle is not against flesh and blood, but against the rulers, against the authorities, against the powers of this dark world and against the spiritual forces of evil in the heavenly realms" (Eph 6:11-12).

These spiritual forces of evil are not human; they are demonic spirits. To withstand their attacks we must depend on God's strength and use what he has given us for our protection. As we have to begun to see in the introduction, demonic spirits are not fantasies—they are very real. Their sole purpose is to destroy our relationship with our loving, merciful God. Although we are assured of victory through Jesus Christ, we still engage in a daily warfare—a spiritual battle. We need the supernatural power of God that comes to us through Jesus Christ through the Holy Spirit to defeat the onslaught of Satan and his demonic spirits.

If I deny the reality of demonic spirits expressed in the Bible, then there is no need for spiritual warfare. And if there is no place of eternal damnation (hell), then there is a lack of sufficient motivation for living a moral life. Without a faith perspective that encompasses the belief in demonic spirits, we will not recognize the need for being involved in any kind of spiritual warfare.

If there are demonic spirits and we do not wish to believe in them, we are left unprotected. Satan can attack us whenever he wants, and we will be susceptible to his attack because we will have no defenses. But if we do believe in demonic spirits, we can be prepared for such attacks. It is through our reliance on the promises of God that we derive strength to be active participants in this spiritual battle. It is our faith in God, relying on his promises, that gives us the victory in this battle because "if God is for us, who can be against us?... In all these things we are more than conquerors through him who loved us" (Rom 8:31, 37).

WHAT IS FAITH?

I remember getting excited when I was growing up as my birthday approached. I was excited because I knew that I would get gifts and other special things. Sometimes there would be surprises. My birthday combined assurance and anticipation. I had faith that my family would get me presents for my birthday. It was a conviction based on past experiences. Faith in God is the conviction that God is present in my life. "Faith is being sure of what we hope for and certain of what we do not see" (Heb 11:1).

As we have seen, faith is a gift from God; it is only by the grace of God that a person can believe (Eph 2:8-9). The apostles believed in Jesus as the Messiah because God the Father had given them the grace to believe (Jn 6:64). Faith is also a human choice. Through faith, people freely choose to submit to the saving love of God. This submission to God's love is expressed through obedience to his Word (Rom 1:5).

The conviction of God's dwelling with me in my life has developed over many years. It was not something that happened instantaneously. Faith has been an ongoing process. In Mark 9:14-29, there is the story of Jesus casting a demon out of a possessed boy. A father had brought his son to Jesus, yet he still doubted Jesus could heal him. He said, "But if you can do anything, take pity on us and help us" (Mk 9:22). Jesus did heal the boy. In this miracle he challenged the father of the boy and the other people present to believe in him. No matter how much faith people have, they never reach the point of being self-sufficient. A Christian grows daily in faith as his or her relationship with God grows.

The apostles asked Jesus to increase their faith (Lk 17:5). Paul thanks God that the Thessalonians' faith and love continue to grow (2 Thes 1:3). Faith cannot be stagnant; if it stagnates, it will die completely. Faith is dynamic and must grow in the life of the believer. As faith grows, one experiences a greater union with God.

In the Old Testament, Abraham's faith grew. God promised to make his descendants into a great nation. Abraham, for his part, was to obey God. The promise was not fulfilled immediately; Abraham's faith in this promise of God was tested. First, there was a famine in his land, so he went to Egypt. In Egypt he became afraid that he would be killed because his wife Sarah was very beautiful. Then Abraham endured family problems with his nephew Lot.

Abraham and Lot parted, and God led Abraham to Hebron, where God again promised to make Abraham's descendants into a great nation. Abraham was old, but God promised him a son. Finally his wife, Sarah, conceived and bore Isaac. The testing of Abraham's faith came to a climax when he was asked to sacrifice this son of the promise. Abraham had learned the lesson of faith well and was obedient—his faith was now seasoned and strong. He believed that somehow God would be faithful to his promise, and so he was. He did not allow Abraham to sacrifice Isaac. God blessed Abraham for his obedience and made his descendants into a great nation—the Jewish people.

Abraham's life is an example of tested faith. His faith grew as he experienced the power of God. He had difficulties, but in his difficulties he did not turn away from God. The apostle James encourages the believer to the true, tested faith of Abraham. This faith is seen in actions. "What good is it, my brothers, if a man claims to have faith but has no deeds?" (Jas 2:14). A Christian's belief in God is expressed through his or her words and actions in the world.

Just because a person believes in God does not mean that he or she will not experience problems. The prophet Jeremiah was a person of great faith. What happened to him? He was attacked for speaking God's Word. He was thrown into the cistern of Malkijah and left there to die (Jer 38:6), but God rescued him. Similarly, in the Book of Daniel, three Jews refused to worship the god of Nebuchadnezzar and were thrown into a fiery furnace. But God saved them from death.

In New Testament times, the apostles were persecuted for proclaiming Jesus as the Messiah. In the first three centuries of the church's history, many followers of Christ were killed for refusing to renounce their faith in Christ. They are called the martyrs of the early church. All of these people trusted in Jesus Christ. Faith did not stop them from suffering. Instead, their faith gave them the strength to witness to the power of Jesus in their lives, even if it meant dying for him.

The goal of faith is our salvation (1 Pt 1:9), which is a gift from God. It is impossible to earn salvation. This gift comes from the redemption brought by the suffering, death, and resurrection of Jesus Christ (Rom 3:23-26). But in order to be saved by the act of Christ's death and resurrection, a person must first affirm the reality of this mystery and freely accept the salvation that God has established and revealed in his Son.[1]

RECEIVING FAITH

How does a person get the gift of faith? As we have seen, we do not earn faith. The Book of Sirach states: "The beginning of wisdom is fear of the Lord, which is formed with the faithful in the womb" (Sir 1:12). The author speaks of true wisdom, God's external revelation of himself. The fear of the Lord means reverence for God. This verse means that God reveals himself and places a reverence for his holy name in a person when he or she is still in the womb. After birth this faith is to be nurtured by the person's family.

My parents nurtured the gift of faith that I received when I was yet unborn. My parents then sent me to St. Catherine of Siena Catholic Parochial School for eight years. I remember that when I came home from school, my mom would be sitting in the rocking chair, praying her rosary. Seeing my mom pray taught me that it was important. My dad made sure that we went to Sunday Mass together as a family. On Christmas Day my brothers and I would not be able to open our presents until we went to Mass.

In our home there was a crucifix or a picture of Jesus or Mary in every room. Our neighbors bought the house next to us because we were "good Catholics." My parents, through their prayers and actions, showed me that God is important in life. I learned to pray, not just from school classes, but from their example at home. Gradually I felt that God was calling me to be a priest. In sixth grade I made a decision that after I graduated from eighth grade, I would enter Our Lady Queen of Angels High School Seminary.

God has touched my life. I did nothing to earn his love; I did nothing to earn the gift of faith. God, in his great love, freely gave me this gift. He has given this gift to all of us. I was very blessed that God placed me in a family that believed in him. God, in his divine providence, gave me everything that I needed to be who I am today. All I have is a gift from him.

THE ATTACK ON FAITH

Yet it is possible to lose one's faith. In the Gospel of Matthew, Jesus warns people that anyone who turns children away from the faith will receive severe punishment (Mt 18:5-7). In examining the world today, it looks like people need to heed this warning from Jesus.

Media and culture. It can be very challenging to hold on to one's faith in today's prevailing moral climate. Look at the scandal that has been spread by the media. Catholic priests and Protestant ministers have been attacked by the media in sensationalistic accounts of sins by the clergy—especially the sin of pedophilia. Thus, reputations are seriously damaged even when the accused are later proven innocent, and the credibility of Christianity is undermined.

In my opinion, many of the leaders of the media wish to destroy true Christianity because it will not follow the morality that the media profess—the media state that abortion is a right; and promotes premarital sex. Through various programs in high schools, teenagers are told it is up to them whether to have sexual relations before marriage, (so long as they use condoms to protect themselve from AIDS). The Catholic Church and other faithful churches disagree.

Do we encourage people to say no to drugs and then give them a needle in case they want to "shoot up"? No! Then what message are we giving our young people when respected educators tell them the dangers of premarital sex and then pass out condoms since "they're just going to have sex anyway"? Talk about a mixed message!

Eighty-three percent of the people in control of the media

believe that the practice of homosexuality is morally permissible as an alternate lifestyle. Some in the media even promote homosexual unions as the equivalent of heterosexual marriage. The Catholic Church and most Protestant churches say no to both. The Catholic Church states that homosexual orientation is not in itself sinful. Homosexual activity, however, like heterosexual activity outside of marriage, is sinful. Because of the Catholic Church's beliefs, the media try to destroy its credibility through sensationalizing scandals. Have you noticed that when a priest or bishop is accused of wrongdoing like pedophilia, the story usually appears on the front page? If they are proved innocent, however, the follow-up story is many times relegated to the back pages.

Another erosion of faith is taking place in our country. Our political leaders have abused the trust of the people. If I bounce a check, I will be liable and have to pay penalties. But when politicians bounce checks, as in the federal banking scandal of 1992, little or nothing happens to them. They remain in office and they are not held liable for their actions. Some of our political leaders are even accused of sexual misconduct, alcoholism, and drug addiction. Yet many of them manage to remain in office.

Family life is falling apart. The statistics show that the rate of divorce is rising. With our continuing high unemployment, it is more difficult for families to survive. Many single-parent families are struggling to provide basic necessities for children. In families with two parents, because both usually have to work, the children are home alone. Who is taking care of them? Who is teaching them right from wrong? Is it any surprise then that more people are living together until they feel that they no longer love each other? There is little if any commitment to many relationships in society. Pornography and prostitution continue to run rampant—exploiting women and children as objects instead of persons. Even *Sports Illustrated* and other mainstream sports magazines offer sexual titillation to men through their annual swimsuit issues. Meanwhile, latchkey children who are home alone watch what can only be characterized as "soft porn" on MTV.

Almost every movie that is not rated "G" has some sex scenes or obscenity, while sex on network TV has become even more explicit. The Hollywood media are trying to erode the morality of our country. "If it feels good, do it" is the current philosophy of life among our youth. A *Los Angeles Times* article (March 25, 1993) interviewed teenagers about sexual relationships. Many of the teenagers said that having sex was just like eating—just as people need food to live, they need to have sex in order to enjoy life. The sexual exploits of nine Lakewood High School boys demonstrate how low the morals for some teenagers in the Los Angeles school system have sunk. These students competed to see how many notches they could cut on their belts (sygnifying how many girls they'd had sex with). According to a study released in 1992 by the Centers for Disease Control, 54 percent of United States students in grades nine through twelve have had sex—and 70 percent of high school seniors. What has happened to morality?

Losses in life. Personal tragedy or loss influences each of our lives. Death and sickness can shake one's faith. In the Gospel of Luke, Jesus gives the example of a man who builds his house upon a firm foundation. The floods came against that house, but it did not fall. He also talks about a house built on sand. The floods came against that house and destroyed it. One's faith can be shaken and destroyed by the problems of life. One's faith can be especially shaken by personal tragedies and losses. Why did this accident happen? Why does God allow me to suffer? Why did I (or a member of my family) get this terminal illness? These catastrophes can shake one's faith. Sometimes people lose their belief in God because of the afflictions they experience. A person's faith must be built upon a firm foundation in order to survive these struggles.

False teachings and philosophy. False teachings can lead people into doubting their belief in the God of the Bible and Christian tradition. A popular movement that spreads false teachings is the New Age Movement.[2] The New Age Movement is best understood as a network, an extremely large, loosely structured collection of organizations and individuals bound together by a common vision.[3] The people in this movement do not believe in the God that is revealed in the Bible. They believe that God is an impersonal energy source.[4]

Current philosophy attacks the belief in God. For example, Communism attacks the beliefs of Christianity. In Vietnam, with the takeover of the Communist Party, there was widespread persecution of Christians. The state became God. Anyone who disagreed with the ideas of the leadership was persecuted or killed. The history of the Communist takeover of Russia and the succeeding years of Communist rule demonstrate the attack of the people of this philosophy upon the Catholic and Protestant churches. Communist repression still continues in China and North Korea.

A current philosophy in the United States that attacks belief in God is secular humanism. Humanism is the human capacity to control the universe and to solve problems through human ingenuity. This happens through technology and the search for knowledge. There are, of course, different forms of humanism. Secular humanism is a type of humanism that exaggerates this capacity to control the universe to the point of denying the presence of God. In secular humanism, the human being is placed at the center of all things, apart from God. Secular humanists in effect believe that Christianity is outmoded. The *Humanist Manifesto II* states:

> As we approach the twenty-first century, however, an affirmative and hopeful vision is needed.... As in 1933 humanists still believe that traditional theism, especially faith in the prayer-hearing God, assumed to love and care for persons, to hear and understand their prayers, and to be able to do something about them is an unproved and outmoded faith. Salvation, based on mere affirmation, still appears as harmful, diverting people with false hopes of heaven hereafter. Reasonable minds look to other means for survival.[5]

Secular humanists wish to destroy Christianity. Belief in God is incompatible with their agenda. They oppose the rights of

Christian parents to educate their children in conformity with the gospel. Their influence is seen in the United States where action is being taken to require that mandatory sex education programs in public schools present premarital sex, homosexuality, and mastur- bation as valid "lifestyle options." Certain features of these pro- grams even encourage sexual experimentation by requiring children to "role play" different types of sexual behavior.[6] In March 1993, a CBS *60 Minutes* television program examined a New York school district where teachers were required to teach kindergarten and first-grade students that homosexual lifestyles are valid options. Such programs are flagrant attacks on the rights of Christian parents to form their children according to their values.

Psychology. Some schools of psychology have tried to deny the reality of God. Other schools of psychology express the impor- tance of self-fulfillment. This theory can lead to a rationalization of Christian values. "Those who think of themselves as practicing Christians, when they are faced with a conflict between self-fulfill- ment and the higher order of Christian values, will generally adopt the rationalization: 'I can't do it.' It sounds better than saying, 'I won't do it.'"[7]

There are even movements to "psychologize" the gospel in Christian universities and seminaries today. They reinterpret the gospel in purely psychological terms. Some people hold to a cer- tain set of beliefs and then reinterpret the Bible to fit their beliefs. Others reject the miracles of Jesus in the Gospels. They state that these are only stories and that they never really happened. Others go so far as to deny the resurrection of Jesus. Biblical truths that have been taught by Catholic and Protestant churches for cen- turies are under attack from "learned" men and women.

Other falsehoods. "If you cannot prove it, then don't believe it"—that is the motto of our materialistic society. Everything, even belief in God, must be empirically proven.

Our society also encourages greed. One television commercial states that you only go around once in life, so grab for all the gusto you can—bigger houses, more cars, more of everything I can get for *me*. Self-gratification is the ultimate good that much of the media promote. It does not matter if you cheat, lie, or steal. All that matters is that you acquire more of everything you want. Yet it never ultimately satisfies, and you always end up wanting more.

But such falsehood and confusion is not limited to the media and the secular sphere. Some priests and theologians have been teaching falsehoods. One theologian was not permitted to teach at a Catholic university because of his controversial teachings. Another priest, after being silenced by the Vatican for one year, was dismissed from his religious order because he refused to follow his vows of obedience to his religious order. The issue of the ordination of women to the priesthood has also brought division to the Catholic Church. Some groups of religious sisters have even banded together to celebrate "a Eucharistic service" without a priest stating that they have the power to change the bread and wine into the Body and Blood of Christ.

It can be difficult to hold onto one's faith in the midst of such a philosophical, emotional, political, and spiritual assault. Sometimes we believers may feel like Peter in the Gospel of Matthew: as their boat was being tossed about by waves Peter saw Jesus walking toward them. Peter called out, "Lord, if it's you, tell me to come to you on the water." Peter, having faith in Jesus, left the boat to meet Jesus, but he became afraid. He began to doubt; he started sinking. In desperation he cries out, "Lord, save me!" Jesus hears his plea (Mt 14:25-32).

We believers, like Peter, are walking toward Jesus. Like Peter, we may begin to be afraid. We may doubt the power and love of God, sinking amidst the storms of the world. We become confused. Our faith is shaken—perhaps, almost lost. Like Peter, we must cry out, "Lord, save me!" Only when we focus on Jesus Christ will we be able to survive the attack of the worldly philosophies and falsehoods around us. We must remember that the wisdom of the world, with all its empty promises, cannot compare to the wisdom of God.

FOR THOSE WHO LACK FAITH

If a person can only receive salvation by affirming the death and resurrection of Jesus Christ and freely accepting the salvation that God has established and revealed in his Son, how can those who are ignorant of Jesus Christ receive salvation? Everyone is touched by the grace of God (Sir 1:12). Because of the universal love of God, every human being receives the grace to believe God's direct self-communication in Jesus Christ.[8] The revelation of the saving love of God may not come to the person during his or her earthly life. This revelation may happen at the point of death. Whether it be in this world or after death, every person must come to a saving knowledge of Jesus Christ because "no one knows who the Son is except the Father, and no one knows who the Father is except the Son and those to whom the Son chooses to reveal him" (Lk 10:22).

Jesus revealed the Father to the people of his time through his preaching and miracles. He can reveal the Father to people today when they read the Bible, receive the sacraments, and follow church teaching. It is possible to begin to believe in God through reflection on creation by recognizing it as God's handiwork. Sometimes people receive an empowerment of faith when they are evangelized by Christians sharing an experience of God. A personal tragedy can be a means of drawing a person to an experience of faith. I believe that a reflection on one's own death can lead a person to believe in God and an afterlife. For if this world is all that there is, why live? Why live with suffering and pain? God can use many different experiences to awaken the gift of faith in a person. He can use a miraculous cure to plant a seed of faith in someone's heart.

I did not believe in the power of God to physically heal someone through prayer until I witnessed it myself. In September 1983, the leaders of our parish prayer group and I went to a healing service given by a priest from Boston. The service was at the Culver City auditorium. During that service I saw a person who was paralyzed get out of his wheelchair and walk. Now I believe in the power of God to heal through prayer. "Blessed are those who have not seen and yet have believed" (Jn 20:29).

PRAYER FOR FAITH

There will be times when our faith may be shaken. At these times we can call out to God to strengthen our faith. We can daily ask him to increase our faith. Remember, when our faith increases, our relationship with God grows. The following is a prayer that can be used to help those who do not believe or to help people in times of difficulty when their faith may be weak:

Heavenly Father, I come before you in humility. I first ask forgiveness for all my doubts that I have about you. Forgive me for doubting your presence and your love in my life. Forgive me for doubting your protection of my life. Forgive me for doubting that you hear my prayers.

I acknowledge that you are the only God. Forgive me for placing other gods above you. Forgive me for placing myself and my worldly desires above you.

The apostles prayed "increase our faith." Today I pray "increase my faith. Increase my faith that I may believe in your love for me. Increase my faith that I may know your power in my life. Increase my faith that I may accept your divine will for my life."

I praise and thank you Father, Son, and Holy Spirit for hearing this prayer. I open myself to you to receive your love. Be my protector and my guide. I pray this prayer through Jesus my Lord in union with the Holy Spirit. Amen.

Even though someone's faith in God may be very strong, he or she may still experience some doubts. What is the source of these intermittent doubts that seem to come out of nowhere? These doubts may not be caused by the assault of the world on faith in God. They may come from another source. Who may be the perpetrator of these questionings of the love and power of God? And who is the spiritual agent behind the assault on the Catholic Church by the world?

TWO

Is Satan Real?

I s there a personal and malevolent spiritual being that is at the root of much of the evil in the world? If so, can this spiritual entity influence people's lives, whether that influence be direct or indirect?

Is Satan a reality, or is he make-believe? This is a very important question. As stated in the previous chapter, if we deny the reality of Satan, then he has free rein. And that is precisely what has happened. This is the only age in the history of Christianity where the presence of Satan is actively being denied by so many—even by members of the clergy. This has led to a crisis of faith and a crisis in morality. My moral theology teacher in the seminary went so far as to state that there is no such thing as the Devil.

The denial of Satan is precisely what he wants. If he is denied, he is able to gain access to our minds. We won't even be aware of what is happening. Little by little we will become more amoral, more evil, more prone to follow our own will and not the will of God. His guerrilla warfare will be out in the open, yet we will not realize it. The constant teaching tradition of the Bible and the Catholic faith in the reality of an evil being, Satan, is crucial to our existence here on earth and in the world to come.

The psalmist states that we are fearfully, wonderfully made (Ps 139:14). This is true. We are works of art. We have wonderfully creative minds. The human race is extremely gifted with tremendous abilities to rule over all creation. But like all good gifts, all our talents can be abused.

At times we can be like little children, asserting our independence from God yet knowing that we are dependent on him. And like that little child who becomes too independent from his or her parent and gets hurt, when we become too independent from God and deny the teaching of the Bible regarding the Devil, we can get ourselves in deep trouble. We have a tendency to assert our beliefs over the Word of God. We desire total autonomy and independence. But our human wisdom is not equal to the wisdom of God. God's wisdom far surpasses human wisdom. God's wisdom is a secret, hidden wisdom that only the Spirit fully comprehends (1 Cor 2:6-11).

In early 1991, the ABC television program *20/20* televised an exorcism, a casting out of a devil that had possessed someone.[1] At the conclusion of this show there was a debate between two Catholic priests, Fr. James LeBar and Fr. Richard McBrien. In this debate Fr. McBrien stated that there was no being called Satan (the Devil). He stated that Satan is only a personification of evil. All evil is due to human decisions. Fr. LeBar argued that belief in Satan is part of the faith of the Catholic Church. Even though much evil is caused by people's choices, Satan can affect human lives and cause evil in the world.

Who is correct? Whose worldview is the truth? Is evil only the result of human choices? Or is there another agent at work in the world? Is belief in Satan an old-fashioned superstition? Or is there a personal spiritual being whose goal is to bring destruction and chaos to human beings?

There are three possible sources for the evil and suffering we have in our world. One is that evil happens to us because of our human condition. We are imperfect beings and have limitations. Because of our limitations we have physical and emotional sufferings which we consider evil. For example, a serious physical or mental sickness can bring great suffering. The cause of the sickness is our human limitations.

The second cause of evil and suffering can be attributed to our free will, our freedom to choose good or evil. For example, when the famine that hit Ethiopia in the mid-1980s resulted in mass starvation, people from many other countries generously donated food and other provisions. The leaders of Ethiopia responded to this kindness by placing an unjust tariff on the food, hoping to raise money to buy weapons. They refused to give in to the needs of their people, and whole families starved as the food rotted on barges. This was an evil that was caused by the free choice of people in power.

A third source of evil is the effect of demonic spirits upon people. This is demonstrated in the stories of possession in the Bible and in history. But demonic spirits can do more than simply oppress or even possess particular individuals. They can affect people's minds and enhance their propensity to do evil in the world. I do not believe that the famine in Ethiopia was solely the act of the leaders. I believe that demonic forces were influencing the leaders and empowering them to do a greater evil than humanly possible. This has happened repeatedly in history. The reign of Hitler and the Holocaust in Germany does not seem to be solely the will of fallen humanity. The magnitude of evil involved is too horrific to be explained purely in human terms. But if I deny the reality of demonic spirits, then all evil and suffering is caused by either our human state or people's choices. And if evil is solely caused by our human condition, how does that square with a just and loving God who made everything good?

Which position is correct? Are there demonic spirits that can affect our lives, or is there no such being as Satan? This question is vital to our understanding of God, our relationship to God, morality, and life after death.

The answer to these questions involves much study, prayer, and observation of human behavior. The starting point is determining the makeup of a human being. A person is a combination of body, mind, and spirit. People have physical bodies with limits. They also have an intelligence—an ability to reason—that separates them from the animals of the world. That part is the human mind.

A human person has something special within him or her as well. It calls the person into an experience with a transcendent reality. This is the spirit of the person. In Catholic theology this spirit is the immortal soul. The immortal soul is directed toward God.

The Book of Sirach states that when a person is conceived, God establishes a relationship with that person. God places a reverence for his holy name within each person when he or she is yet unborn (Sir 1:12). According to the Bible, this integral part of a person is meant to be in relationship to God.

It is important for people to be aware of these three parts of the human being. If any one part is excluded, it produces a diminished view of humanity. When a person is seeking counseling, for example, in order to help with the problems of life, the whole person—body, mind, and spirit—must be explored and understood. It is essential for therapists to understand all parts of the person who has come to them for help.

EVIL AND ITS EFFECTS

Recently I spoke with a therapist. She is involved in a program that helps adult victims of child abuse. In her counseling sessions with some patients she noticed something peculiar. She believed in God, but did not practice any specific religion. The more she worked with her patients, however, the more she realized that something strange was occurring with a couple of them. Their experiences of child abuse had a different character than those of other cases. There was something sinister and evil in them.

This evil was so horrible that she could not explain it with psychology. Many evils of the world can be explained with the help of modern psychology. Much evil can be directly attributed to choices that people make, but another kind of evil has a more sinister and diabolical character.

She shared this with some of her colleagues. They were experiencing the same thing in some sessions with other adult victims of child abuse. The evil could not be sufficiently explained by psychology alone.

The evil that this therapist (and many others) have uncovered is a destructive, sinister evil. This evil tries to destroy the very heart of its victims. The abuse that these victims suffer is an attack on all levels of the human person—physical, emotional, mental, and spiritual. This abuse is performed in the name of a spiritual being—Satan. Psychology alone cannot explain this evil. The history of the human race does not sufficiently explain this evil. In all of the books that have been written, the Bible has the most reasonable explanation of how this evil can be explained.

There is a growing awareness of ritual abuse in today's society—the kind of abuse that many of these victims suffered from in childhood. The broadcast media has carried special reports on this type of abuse, which cannot be separated from its spiritual component because it is done in the name of Satan. The perpetrators of this abuse believe that they are in contact with Satan, through whom they wish to receive power.

They perform atrocities on innocent children in order to snuff out the life of God in the child. They wish to implant an evil self-concept, so that these children will commit evil when they are adults. They also desire that some of their victims return and join their satanic cults when they are adults. They try to brainwash innocent children into accepting their belief system—a belief system that proclaims Satan as the lord and ruler of the universe.

You may be surprised to learn that the practice of Satanism is steadily rising among teenagers. Just examine the proliferation of books that describe how to perform satanic rituals in the occult sections in bookstores. Anyone can perform a ritual, they just need the proper incantations and an animal (or human being) for their sacrifice. Satanism is not just a fad, it is serious business. It is growing to be a multi-million dollar business, just like pornography.

Our society has seen fit to remove prayer from our public schools. We have omitted God from our vocabulary in most public discourse, and some people have even tried to take the phrase "in God we trust" off our currency. Except in the context of church and religious organizations, the name of God is seldom uttered anymore. Our society has created a spiritual vacuum.

Sadly, many church leaders and Christian parents are following suit. They are not teaching the basics of faith in God and Christian morality to our children. And when God is not proclaimed as Lord and Ruler of the universe, even among his own people, Satan is ready, waiting in the wings to take over.

Recent history should tell us that if we forsake God the human race will turn to evil. And there is something greater than human evil at work in the world to turn us away from God. We can see it today in the terrible atrocities in Bosnia-Herzegovina and Somalia—to name but a few.

The Bible tells us such diabolical evil originated with the revolt of a heavenly angel called Satan, as we see in the Revelation passage cited early in the introduction.

SATAN IS A FALLEN ANGEL OPPOSED TO GOD

This passage of Scripture makes clear that Satan is an angelic being—evil is not simply a lack of human goodness in the world. "The Devil... is not to be regarded as a mere mythological personification of evil in the world; the existence of the Devil cannot be denied."[2]

The proper name "Satan" first appears in Job 1:6-12, where Satan asks God's permission to roam the earth and to test Job (and by implication, other followers of the Lord). Satan is not equal to God. He must ask permission from God. Satan is a created being and is subservient to the Creator, God. He, with his followers, fell away from God and were thrust out of heaven.[3] Now he "prowls around like a roaring lion looking for someone to devour" (1 Pt 5:8).

The Jewish people believed that there were evil spirits. In Leviticus 16:6-10, *azazel*, according to most scholars, is both the Hebrew word for "desert" and the name of the demon who lives there.[4] In the Hebrew tradition, evil forces are not to be appeased. The people of God were to give honor to the only true God. All contact with evil or demonic forces was explicitly forbidden. The Hebrew prophets repeatedly described other religions as demon-controlled and insisted that any dalliance with them is idolatry.[5] Consulting with the gods of pagan nations or demonic forces, in Hebrew thought, was a very serious offense against the Lord. "But the angel of the Lord said to Elijah the Tishbite, 'Go up and meet the messengers of the king of Samaria and ask them, "Is it because there is no God in Israel that you are going off to consult Baal-Zebub, the god of Ekron?" Therefore this is what the Lord says: "You will not leave the bed you are lying on. You will certainly die!"' So Elijah went" (2 Kgs 1:3-4).

So we see that in the Old Testament the Devil, Satan, is a reality. He was allowed to test Israel's faithfulness to God, but did not possess the same power as that of the Lord. God alone was sovereign and his will was to be obeyed. God called Israel to "be holy, because I am the Lord your God" (Lv 20:7).

Satan in the New Testament. In the New Testament we receive a clearer understanding of the role of Satan. Jesus' earthly ministry demonstrates that he—that is, God in the flesh—came to free us from our sins and the grasp of Satan.

In the Gospels of Matthew, Mark, and Luke, Jesus is prepared for his public ministry through his Baptism in the Jordan River. In this act Jesus is revealed as the leader of the new people of God who are to find their identity as sons and daughters of the Father. In Baptism Jesus united himself with sinful humanity. He then began his ministry by a confrontation with Satan, known as the forty days of temptation in the desert. Jesus, full of the Holy Spirit, engages Satan on his own battleground and is the faithful witness (Rv 1:5) who is loyal to the Father (Mk 1:12-13; Mt 4:1-11; Lk 4:1-13).

After this victory, the Gospel of Mark indicates that Jesus called the first disciples. The Gospel of Luke states that Jesus began to teach. In these Gospels the first sign (healing or miracle) of the power of Jesus is the casting out of a demonic spirit:

> Just then a man in their synagogue who was possessed by an evil spirit cried out, "What do you want with us, Jesus of Nazareth? Have you come to destroy us? I know who you are—the Holy One of God!"
>
> "Be quiet!" said Jesus sternly. "Come out of him!" The evil spirit shook the man violently and came out of him with a shriek.
>
> The people were all so amazed that they asked each other, "What is this? A new teaching—and with authority! He even gives orders to evil spirits and they obey him." **Mark 1:23-27**

Since Jesus' first act is to confront Satan in the desert and the first sign of Jesus' power and authority is the casting out of a demonic spirit, it appears that a primary purpose of Jesus' ministry was to expose Satan's activity and destroy his power. Jesus' victory—which can be ours—is completed with his death and resurrection, and then coupled with God's sending of the Holy Spirit.

Further, this authority over evil spirits is integral to Jesus' ministry and not a rare occurrence. He casts out demonic spirits many times in the Gospels, each time bringing freedom and healing to a person. According to the Gospels, the demonic spirits of Satan are real. If they were not, Jesus would not have dealt with them as such. In fact, I believe that to deny the existence of Satan and his demonic spirits is to deny the truthfulness of the Bible, the inspired Word of God. After all, Satan plays a significant role in salvation history, in both the Old and New Testaments. The Bible, according to Vatican II, faithfully teaches us what we need to know for our salvation, and Satan is an important part of the revelation. From Genesis to Revelation, he is not incidental to it.

And what of our view of Jesus himself if we deny the existence of Satan? Aren't we then questioning a significant part of Jesus' earthly ministry as recorded in the Gospels? At the very least, we must question Jesus' apparent understanding of these dark forces as demonic. For if they were merely physical or psychological in origin, this would show a lack of understanding, even ignorance, on his part. He evidently treated demons as if they were real. He differentiated between simply healing the sick and casting out demons. What happens then to our conception of Jesus as the Son of God?

Affirming the Gospels, the Catholic Church in every age has believed in demonic spirits who are directed by a powerful, personal being: Satan. He wishes to draw humanity away from the power and love of God the Father. The early church fathers were concerned to protect Christians and those preparing for

Baptism from these satanic influences. They believed that the church was to continue the ministry of Jesus. The proclamation of the kingdom of God included deliverance from the work of evil spirits. Justin Martyr writes that the ministry of healing and casting out of evil spirits follows the example of Jesus and that Christians are able to defeat the enemy through the power of Jesus' name.[6]

As the gospel was preached in the early church, it was a given that Jesus' proclamation would be met with resistance from the Evil One. An integral part of the church's proclamation included prayers for healing and deliverance from evil spirits. St. Iraneus writes that those who follow Jesus receive a special grace which empowers them to drive out demonic spirits so that people may be cleansed from evil, and thus be prepared to be received into the church through Baptism.[7]

It is evident that the early church waged war against evil spirits through individual and collective prayer. St. Ignatius of Antioch wrote to the Ephesians that they were to come together often and praise God, and thereby defeat Satan. Being a Christian meant joining Jesus in warfare against the Devil.[8]

In the early church, a person wishing to be baptized was prepared through receiving a series of exorcisms which took place after the candidates registered their names.[9] Also the prayer of casting out of evil spirits was common. Through the wisdom imparted by the Holy Spirit, the first Christians understood what Jesus was doing when he cast out evil spirits in the Gospels, and they believed that they were to continue this work. The theologian Origen emphasizes the power of a simple prayer against Satan using the name of Jesus. He reminded people that Jesus encouraged his followers to use the authority of his name. He teaches that when a follower of Jesus commands an evil spirit to flee, it must leave.[10]

THE CHURCH'S ABIDING BELIEF

The belief in the existence of the Devil and demonic spirits does not end with the early years of the Catholic Church. The Fourth Lateran Council (A.D. 1215) states: "For the Devil and the other demons were indeed created by God naturally good, but they became evil by their own doing. As for man, he sinned at the suggestion of the Devil."[11]

The Second Vatican Council repeats this teaching in several documents. The "Dogmatic Constitution on the Church" teaches that Satan is the one who deceives human beings and leads them away from God.[12] The "Constitution on the Sacred Liturgy" teaches that Jesus through his death and resurrection freed humanity from the power of Satan.[13] In the "Decree on the Church's Missionary Activity" the Council teaches that Jesus was sent to rescue humanity from the power of darkness, thereby reconciling the world to God.[14]

The church sends forth missionaries to free all people from bondage to Satan and restore all of creation to the lordship of Jesus Christ.[15] The "Pastoral Constitution on the Church in the Modern World" states that Jesus was crucified and rose in order to break the hold that Satan had on the world. Through his death and resurrection, the world can be made new, according to the plan of God.[16]

It is evident, from the Council's teaching, that my moral theology teacher at seminary was wrong. There is a being called Satan—a being not equal with God, but subject to God. Evil is not simply a lack of human goodness. Real personal evil exists beyond the human realm. Followers of Christ are in a daily struggle against "the rulers, against the authorities, against the powers of this dark world and against the spiritual forces of evil in the heavenly realms" (Eph 6:12).

Pope Paul VI in a general audience on November 15, 1972 even went so far as to state that one of the greatest needs of the

Catholic Church at the present time was to be aware of Satan. "This matter of the Devil and of the influence he can exert on individuals as well on communities, entire societies or events, is a very important chapter of Catholic doctrine which should be studied again, although it is given little attention today."[17]

In its rite of Baptism for children, the Catholic Church expresses its belief in Satan. After the litany of the saints, the priest prays: "Almighty and ever-living God, you sent your only Son into the world to cast out the power of Satan, spirit of evil, to rescue man from the kingdom of darkness, and bring him into the splendor of your kingdom of light. We pray for these children: set them free from original sin, make them temples of your glory, and send your Holy Spirit to dwell within them."[18] Later in the rite of Baptism the parents and godparents are asked to renounce Satan and all his works and machinations.

The Rite for Christian Initiation of Adults (RCIA) also contains prayers of exorcism that adults are to receive before being baptized. These are intended to free them from sin, free them from the Devil, and to give them strength in Christ, who is the Way, the Truth, and the Life: "Never let the powers of evil deceive them. Free them from the spirit of falsehood and help them recognize any evil within themselves.... In your love, free them from evil.... Command the spirit of evil to leave them, for you have conquered that spirit by rising to life."[19]

In 1975, the Sacred Congregation for the Doctrine of the Faith published "Les Formes de la Superstition" to help the faithful to understand the Catholic Church's teaching regarding demonic spirits. Satan, it states, is not a product of the human imagination, but a real historical figure first described in the Bible and a key person in church doctrine. When someone says, "There is no Satan," one is denying the constant faith of the Catholic Church, its way of conceiving redemption, and the very consciousness of Jesus himself.[20] To deny the existence of evil spirits is to deny, at least in part, the need for redemption which Jesus brought us through his death and resurrection. After all, an important component of that redemption is our deliverance from the Evil One, not only deliverance from sin and death.

The Catholic Church has taught for two thousand years the reality of an evil being, Satan. The Bible states that Satan is a reality. Yet, when was the last time that you heard a sermon in church about Satan? Why has this constant teaching of our faith been silent over the past years? Because many of the leaders of the church have bought the lie—the lie that Satan is either nonexistent or not powerful, that a sinister outside force does not influence our decisions.

The leaders have bought the lie of psychology. Psychology is good and helpful, but when psychology draws us away from a revealed truth, then it promotes a lie. And modern psychology refuses to accept the presence of an evil reality distinct from ourselves that can influence our decisions. It believes that all evil is human in origin. As long as many of our church leaders buy into that lie, the truth will not be proclaimed.

We have also bought the lie because of Satan himself. He desires that we forget about him. He does not want to be noticed. He loves to be invisible because then he can move about freely, leading us into sin. But if he is exposed, then he will not have power over us. Ignorance of him and his tactics is his great advantage. And too many of our leaders have allowed him free rein by not teaching the faithful in a balanced and prudent way about his existence and power.

"I will strike the shepherd, and the sheep of the flock will be scattered" (Mt 26:31). Satan has attacked the shepherds of the church. Look at the abuses highlighted in the news: clergy having affairs, clergy dealing in drugs, clergy stealing church money, alcoholism, and even active homosexuality among certain clergy. Satan is striking the shepherds. And the sheep are scattering because they have forgotten how to fight this attack.

We have lived in ignorance for too long. We should earnestly pray that our leaders will begin to stand up and proclaim the truth of the attack of Satan upon the church and the world.

But this proclamation must be balanced and prudent because the other ploy of Satan is that we see him everywhere. There is a tendency to attribute to him every evil that happens. Some evil in the world is caused by human beings, but some evil is the direct result of a personal evil being. And some evil is a combination of the two. We need a balanced and careful approach to spiritual warfare.

CONCLUSION

We can conclude the following:

1. If we want to understand the whole human person, psychological and physical views of personhood are not enough. We must consider the spiritual dimension of the human being.

2. Today, counselors and therapists are discovering that in certain cases of adult victims of child abuse, there is an evil which is so horrible it cannot be explained solely in psychological terms, confirming the need to consider the spiritual dimension and possibly even the activity of supernatural beings. (Obviously, this is only one example of such sinister evil.)

3. The existence of a personal Devil and evil spirits is a credible explanation, at least in part, for such sinister evil in the lives of human beings and the world as a whole.

4. The Bible, especially Jesus in the Gospels, confirms the existence of a personal Devil who is active in the world.

5. In accord with Scripture, the Catholic Church has consistently taught that there is a personal Devil. This teaching is reflected in both the Church's belief and practice.

Satan does exist. Demonic spirits exist. But what are they like? How do they operate in the world? How do they oppress us on earth? And how much power do they have? Since we are involved in spiritual warfare, we must know the enemy.

"Suppose a king is about to go to war against another king. Will he not first sit down and consider whether he is able with ten thousand men to oppose the one coming against him with twenty thousand?" (Lk 14:31). For our own safety, we must not be ignorant of Satan and his army. If we do not know him and his strength we will not be victorious. Our power over Satan lies in knowledge—knowledge of the power given to us by Jesus and knowledge of Satan and his tactics.

So just how powerful is he? And what does he try to do?

THREE

Satan: His Nature and His Activity in the World

For our struggle is not against flesh and blood, but against the rulers, against the authorities, against the powers of this dark world and against the spiritual forces of evil in the heavenly realms. **Ephesians 6:12**

In Ephesians, is all of humanity engaged in a spiritual war? Yes! Christians become soldiers in that battle upon their Baptism.

In combat it is vital to know the enemy. Any good general knows his enemy's strengths and weaknesses. Christians must do the same. So who are Satan and the demons? They are fallen spirits. The good angels are also spirits, but they are not demonic. Some of the good angels are messengers from God.

The archangel Gabriel, for example, was sent to a town of Galilee named Nazareth, to a virgin... the virgin's name was Mary (Lk 1:26-38). Some angels minister to God continually praising his name (Rv 8:2). God sends other angels to assist people in their walk with the Lord (Heb 1:14). The angel

55

Raphael was sent to help Tobiah (Tb 5:4). Demons, on the other hand, are messengers of Satan, their leader.

Angels and demonic spirits act differently. In the Bible, angels do not wish to enter or possess a person or animal. Angels are content to do God's will. Demonic spirits do the opposite. They desire to inhabit or attach themselves to a body, whether a human or an animal, and possess it.

> They went across the lake to the region of the Gerasenes. When Jesus got out of the boat, a man with an evil spirit came from the tombs to meet him.... When he saw Jesus from a distance, he ran and fell on his knees in front of him. He shouted at the top of his voice, "What do you want with me, Jesus, Son of the Most High God? Swear to God that you won't torture me!..."
>
> "My name is Legion," he replied, "for we are many." And he begged Jesus again and again not to send them out of the area.... A large herd of pigs was feeding on the nearby hillside. The demons begged Jesus, "Send us among the pigs; allow us to go into them." **Mark 5:1-12**

The demonic spirits did not want to leave the home they had become accustomed to in the Gerasene demoniac. They begged Jesus to send them into the pigs, thus demonstrating that demonic spirits wish to inhabit or attach to a bodily form, human or animal. If a demonic spirit is cast out and cannot attach to another human or animal, it will try to return to its former place of habitation (Mt 12:43-45).

The angels reside in heaven and follow the will of God. The demonic spirits rebelled against God and either reside in hell or prowl the earth like roaring lions, looking for someone to devour (1 Pt 5:8).

In the Gerasene demoniac passage, one also realizes that demonic spirits have strong wills with which to bargain and struggle against Jesus. Though they resist, in the final analysis they must always be obedient to God's power (Mk 10:17-29).

Demonic spirits also identify with emotions. One emotion expressed in the Gospels is fear (Mk 5:6-7). They have names as well. In the Gerasene story, they are named "Legion." Demonic spirits possess knowledge. In Mark, one demonic spirit shrieks, "What do you want with us, Jesus of Nazareth? Have you come to destroy us? I know who you are—the Holy One of God!" (Mk 1:24).

In Luke, "demons also came out of many people, shouting, 'You are the Son of God!'" (Lk 4:41). Knowing that Jesus was the Son of God, the demons also knew that he had the power to destroy them. So does anyone who is a true follower of Jesus because he or she has received this authority from the Lord.

Acts 19:13-16 shows that it is dangerous to try to use the power of the name of Jesus if one is not following the Lord. The demonic spirits knew the faith of the Jewish exorcists. The demons even spoke to them; the demonic spirits knew who was commanding them to leave. They knew, for example, that these sons of Sceva were not followers of Jesus. On the other hand, they knew that Paul was a true follower of Jesus and had the power to cast them out using Jesus' name (Acts 16:16-18). Demonic spirits can discern if a person is trying to follow the Lord's will with sincere devotion that leads to a deep relationship with him, or if he or she is a lukewarm Christian.

THE BATTLE IS DAILY

The daily struggle to follow the Lord Jesus naturally encompasses a battle against Satan and his demonic forces. Satan does not want a follower of Jesus to live in peace and harmony. Satan declares himself to be god and lord of the earth. His goal is to annihilate the followers of the Lord by seducing them away from God.

Don't let anyone deceive you in any way, for that day will not come until the rebellion occurs and the man of lawlessness is revealed, the man doomed to destruction. He will oppose and will exalt himself over everything that is called God or is worshiped, so that he sets himself up in God's temple, proclaiming himself to be God.

Don't you remember that when I was with you I used to tell you these things? And now you know what is holding him back, so that he may be revealed at the proper time. For the secret power of lawlessness is already at work; but the one who now holds it back will continue to do so till he is taken out of the way. And then the lawless one will be revealed, whom the Lord Jesus will overthrow with the breath of his mouth and destroy by the splendor of his coming. The coming of the lawless one will be in accordance with the work of Satan displayed in all kinds of counterfeit miracles, signs and wonders, and in every sort of evil that deceives those who are perishing. They perish because they refused to love the truth and so be saved. 2 Thessalonians 2:3-10

Though Satan attacks the followers of Jesus in different ways, the Christian must always remember "neither death nor life, neither angels nor demons, neither the present nor the future, nor any powers, neither height nor depth, nor anything else in all creation, will be able to separate us from the love of God that is in Christ Jesus our Lord" (Rom 8:38-39).

For the faithful servants of God, all Satan can do is to harass them and make life difficult. Satan tries to deceive, entice, enslave, torment (bring into bondage), drive people away from God, or defile them even if they are baptized. (All human beings are called to be people of God.) A major tactic of Satan is to attack our minds and thoughts. He wants to deceive us for "there is no truth in him. When he lies, he speaks his native language, for he is a liar and the father of lies" (Jn 8:44). After a person hears the Word of God, "Satan [can come] and [take] away the word that was sown in them" (Mk 4:15).

The main battle is in the mind of the believer. If Satan can control our thoughts, then he can control the actions of a person. Satan does not directly control our intellect or our will. He affects them through our emotions, memories, and imagination. These faculties form our perceptions and beliefs. If Satan can gain access to our mental faculties that deal with our perceptions and beliefs, then he can affect the decisions that we make with our will. We make the decisions, but these decisions are affected by our perceptions and beliefs. Many times the obsessive thoughts that a person experiences are a combination of psychological problems and spiritual infiltration. In order for the person to experience true peace and freedom, both levels must be dealt with (see chapter six).

Satan is a master at attacking our thoughts. That is why it is very important to "take captive every thought and to make it obedient to Christ (2 Cor 10:5). If we wish to dwell on negativity, then our lives will be full of problems. But if we wish to dwell on the positive, the love, forgiveness, and protection of God, we will experience happiness.

Sandra came in to see me one day. She was experiencing many negative thoughts, mostly about her own goodness. She thought that she was an evil woman and she lived her life to demonstrate that self-fulfilling prophecy. She had repented of her sins, but she was unable to let go of her sinful actions. After confessing her sins she would change for a time, but that change was short-lived. The minute she committed one of her past sins, she fell back into the same old pattern of life. Sandra believed that she was forgiven, but she did not forgive herself. That was the lie of Satan. When she fell back into the old pattern of sin, she became depressed, thinking that it was impossible for her to change. She was obsessed with her own problematic behavior.

Many of us can be like Sandra. We confess our sins to the Lord. We follow God's ways, but fall back into the same old sin. And when we fall back into it, we begin to think that we will never change, that it is no use, that we might as well give up. Notice how sneaky Satan is. He starts with one persistent sin and then influences our belief patterns to the degree that we want to give up trying to follow God. Part of the problem is our own attitude that we must be perfect, but a great part of this problem is our believing that it is impossible to change. We believe that this is the way we are.

When we fall into this pattern, we become prey to Satan's tricks. Sandra was finally able to stop her pattern of disbelief when she accepted the grace to forgive herself. When she forgave herself, she was able to experience a deeper filling of God's love and forgiveness. She also was able to stop the cycle of negative thinking.

We too need to forgive ourselves. God created us as human beings. Part of being human is accepting that we are imperfect and limited creations. Accepting our imperfections does not mean that we stop trying to change. Accepting our imperfections does not mean that we accept our sins. Being imperfect means that we realize that we are constantly changing and growing. We can change positively or negatively. We strive to follow the will of God, but we also realize that we will never do the will of God perfectly in this life. That is part of our human condition.

Satan plays on this human condition. He knows how to attack our thoughts. When we accept our humanity, our imperfections, it is possible to grow. Then we realize that we can do nothing by ourselves and that we rest on the power of Jesus Christ to bring about change in us. Jesus does not condemn us in our sinfulness. He forgives us. So too, we should not condemn ourselves for being sinners. Like Jesus, we are to forgive ourselves when we fall. When we forgive ourselves, we are freed from the kind of depression that can lead to destruction.

John came in to see me. Part of his obsessive thought pattern was suicide. He had had suicidal thoughts for many years, but he had never acted on them. But now the thoughts were growing more troublesome. He had been in counseling, but that did not seem to help much. As he talked, I believed that there was a spirit attacking his thoughts, aggravating his depression and negativity. As we prayed, I bound the spirit of death and suicide. In the name of Jesus, I commanded the spirit to leave him and not to return.

After that we prayed for inner healing, to heal the trauma that allowed this and other spirits to attach themselves to him. He felt greatly relieved following our prayer session. John has not had trouble with suicidal thoughts since that day. Blessed be Jesus, our Lord and Healer. He truly does heal the broken and bring deliverance to the captives. He brings us freedom and protection from such destructive thoughts.

Satan leads us down a path of suffering and sorrow. Satan is a liar and a destroyer. Jesus is the Way, the Truth, and the Life (Jn 14:6). In seeking Jesus, we seek the way of peace and happiness which is union with God our Father. We seek the truth, the truth that we are forgiven. Further, we need to accept that because Jesus forgives us, we can forgive ourselves. We seek the life promised by Jesus to his faithful followers. Satan wants to rob us of that life and ultimately seeks our spiritual death. It is very important for us to be ready for his attacks.

The followers of Jesus must always be alert: "The Spirit clearly says that in later times some will abandon the faith and follow deceiving spirits and things taught by demons" (1 Tm 4:1). To withstand the attacks of Satan on the mind, one must become fortified by the Word of God.

Not only does Satan attack our thoughts, he attacks our

physical being as well (Lk 13:10-13, 16). Demonic spirits have the power to affect our senses and physical abilities. In Matthew 12:22-23, Jesus cured the possessed man by removing the spirit that inhabited him. In Mark, a man brings his son to Jesus because the boy is possessed by a mute spirit (Mk 9:17). In Mark, the Syro-Phoenician woman ascribes her daughter's problem to possession by an evil spirit (Mk 7:25-30).

Paul indicates that demonic spirits can harass anyone, even a member or leader in the church (2 Cor 12:7-9). Though the angel of Satan afflicted Paul, God allowed it so that the power of the Lord Almighty would be manifested. Satan also attacks present day church leaders. As we have seen in the last two years, the media have reported several allegations of sexual abuse by church clergy. In addition, we have heard that some ministers and priests are abusing alcohol and drugs. In Los Angeles a church minister was accused of stealing over fifty thousand dollars in church contributions. The drive for power can become very strong and corrupt those in leadership positions, even in our churches. Such abuse can appear to have become rampant as Satan attempts to discredit Christianity and its leaders. We need to recognize these are not simple human problems. Many of our church leaders are being besieged by Satan and need our prayers.

Part of the problem is that when church leaders refuse to acknowledge the reality of demonic spirits, they leave themselves wide open for attack. The difference between St. Paul and much of the present leadership of the churches is that St. Paul knew the presence and power of Satan and the demonic spirits. St. Paul knew how to fight against the powers of evil. Many of our church leaders seem to have forgotten his example in this regard. They have allowed themselves to be attacked through their own vincible ignorance. "I will strike the shepherd, and the sheep will be scattered" (Mk 14:27). Satan is being allowed to strike the shepherds, and the sheep are scattering in confusion.

Satan and his demonic spirits will use any means at their disposal to separate us from God. They will attack our physical bodies. They will attack our emotions. They will attack our thoughts. They will attack our prayer life. They will attack our leaders. Demons will encourage us to doubt the power and love of God. We may feel as if we are alone, with no one to help us in our struggle—our personal agony in the garden. For example, demonic spirits can affect one's mind to the point of even causing mental disorders. Remember that some mental disorders are organic and others are psychological. But some disorders can be the result of demonic attack. A demonic spirit can cause distorted thinking. (But in order for this to be true the person must first go through physical and psychological testing to demonstrate that there are no organic disorders. We must be very careful not to diagnose a spiritual remedy if the problem is fundamentally organic.)

Demons can cause violent reactions in people. The Gerasene man who was oppressed by an evil spirit was violent (Lk 8:26-29). Jesus cured the man by casting out the demons. I was giving a talk about Satan and the occult to a youth group. At the end of the talk, I invited those who wished to come forward for prayer and a blessing. A young man came to me and told me that he had repeated violent thoughts. He never acted out on the thoughts, but they disturbed him. He had recurring urges to kill animals and rip their insides out. He was obsessed with books and movies whose main theme was violence. In silence, I bound the spirit of violence in the name of Jesus and commanded it to leave him. After my quiet prayer, a sense of peace and calm filled this young man. He felt totally different. I cautioned him to stay away from violent books and movies and encouraged him to pursue more wholesome reading.

Demons also can cause bodily disease. Luke 13:10-17 tells

the story of a woman who had been crippled by a demonic spirit for eighteen years. Jesus set her free from her infirmity. In many healing services, people are freed from spirits of infirmity. In praying during a healing service, I often discover that people's backs have been healed when the spirit of infirmity is commanded to leave their **bodies,** go to the cross of Jesus, and not return.

All of Satan's diabolical activity in the world, however, should not make us overly fearful. Remember: Even though Satan is powerful, and even though he has an angelic intellect, he is not all-powerful or all-knowing. There is only one Lord, Jesus Christ who is all-powerful and omniscient. Satan's days are numbered. He is living on borrowed time. Jesus has conquered him for eternity. Our victory over him in Jesus is assured.

A PERSONAL ATTACK

I had been a priest for six years, and I was the associate pastor of St. Brendan Church—my second parish assignment. Even though I was happy, I just did not feel right. There was something in my life that was troubling me. I believed that when I went to confession my sins were forgiven, but I did not feel forgiven. I kept asking myself, "How could I, a priest, have committed that sin?" As I examined my life, I saw my sins and I could not understand how Jesus could forgive me. I felt that I was a terrible sinner, yet here I was leading my parish in Mass. My life was to be an example for them, yet how could it be since I felt like such a terrible sinner.

I would condemn myself for my actions. I would say, "I can do better. How could I have said this or done that?" I would confess my sins, pray the act of contrition, and do my penance, but I experienced no lasting peace. On the outside I looked happy, but inside of me I experienced constant battles about my sinfulness. I was living under a spirit of self-condemnation.

In June of 1986, I went to a priest-deacon conference at the Franciscan University of Steubenville in Ohio. The retreat began on Monday evening. There were over five hundred priests at this retreat. I felt fine during most of the retreat, but as I prayed I felt that something was still missing in my life. I believed that I was a good priest. I had a vibrant prayer life. The people in my parish were happy that I was with them, but something was wrong. Something deep inside was attacking me, gnawing at my life, sucking the joy and peace of God out of me. I was not at peace. I was involved in an internal battle. On Thursday afternoon of the conference something happened to me that changed my life and finally brought me peace.

FOUR

Redemption through Jesus Christ

Fr. Francis Martin gave a presentation on Thursday afternoon. He talked about the power of the Blood of Christ. As he spoke, I became aware that in my mind, I knew of the power of Jesus' death for me, but I did not experience the reality of it in my heart. I knew that I was forgiven, but I did not feel cleansed of sin in my heart. Did I really know the power of the Blood of Christ? Did I realize that by God's estimation I am worth the shedding of the Blood of Christ? I was challenged to accept the truth—that Jesus has washed me clean in his precious Blood.

I wanted to accept righteousness before God on my own terms. That was pride. I was challenged to accept righteousness on God's terms through the saving power of the Blood of Jesus Christ. After that talk I knew that I had to be alone. I was challenged with the truth—the power of the Blood of Christ for my life. I had not invited the power of Christ's Blood to renew every part of my life. There was still a hidden secret—my sinfulness and unworthiness that I felt I had to conquer. I was under a spirit of self-condemnation.

I went to my room to pray. I knelt down beside my bed and concentrated on the crucifix in my room. I prayed, "Heavenly Father, I want to know, at the very depth of my being, the power of the Blood of Jesus Christ for me. I want to believe that I am worth the shedding of the Blood of Christ." Then I opened my Bible to Romans 8:1. Before I read this passage I prayed, "Holy Spirit, reveal this passage of Scripture to me, that I may once and for all, know the power of the Blood of Christ. Help me to let go of my self-condemnation."

I slowly prayed Romans 8:1, "Therefore, there is now no condemnation for those who are in Christ Jesus, because through Christ Jesus the law of the Spirit of life set me free from the law of sin and death." After praying this verse, I begged the Holy Spirit for the full revelation of its meaning. Then I began to experience a great peace.

It was as if a great weight was lifted from my body. I felt a deep, inner peace—a peace that I had never experienced before. Finally I knew the power of the Blood of Christ. I am not condemned; I am in Jesus Christ. He has taken my condemnation to his cross and through his cross I am set free. Finally I knew the truth. Jesus Christ, through his Blood, removed my self-condemnation and healed my life.

In the Stations of the Cross we pray, "We adore you, O Christ, and we praise you, because by your holy cross you have redeemed the world." Yes! The whole world is redeemed through the cross of Jesus Christ! When we fully accept this reality, our lives change forever.

REDEMPTION THROUGH THE BLOOD

We cannot free ourselves from Satan and sin. Jesus is the one who has rescued us from the powers of darkness. "For you know that it was not with perishable things such as silver or gold that you were redeemed from the empty way of life handed down to you from your forefathers, but with the precious blood of Christ, a lamb without blemish or defect" (1 Pt 1:18-19).

The saving Blood of Christ is a gift to us. Just as God chose the people of Israel and cleansed them, so too through the Blood of Christ, God has chosen those who follow him. It was God who brought the Israelites out of Egypt (Ex 6:5-7). The people were holy because God chose them to be his own (Dt 7:6-8). This saving action of God in the Old Testament freed his people so that they could belong entirely to him (2 Sm 7:23).

The shed Blood of Christ claims Christians, for through Jesus' Blood we are "a chosen people, a royal priesthood, a holy nation, a people belonging to God, that you may declare the praises of him who called you out of darkness into his wonderful light" (1 Pt 2:9). In pouring out his Blood, Jesus gave us his own life. In the Old Testament it was through the shedding of blood that a person received atonement. "For the life of a creature is in the blood, and I have given it to you to make atonement for yourselves on the altar; it is the blood that makes atonement for one's life" (Lv 17:11).

Jesus, through shedding his blood, has paid the price for our lives (Acts 20:28). He has freed us from the guilt of sin. He died in our place. His death was the appropriate sacrifice for our transgressions. It is through his cross that we receive pardon, peace, and freedom (Rom 3:25-26). Redemption through the Blood of Jesus Christ covers six areas.

1. **We are reconciled to God through the Blood.** To be reconciled is more than being forgiven. To be reconciled means our relationship is made new. Forgiveness is unilateral; it is something that one can do all by oneself. For example, I do not have to wait for you to ask me to forgive you. I can do

that before you ask. But reconciliation is different. If two people are going to be reconciled, both of them must be involved. I can desire to be reconciled to you, but if you refuse there is nothing I can do but wait. I can hope that your heart will change, but I will have to wait. My sin separated me from God. When I am reconciled by the Blood of Jesus, I am brought back into relationship with God.

2. We are cleansed through the Blood. To be cleansed is to be made clean. Think of it this way: When we have an open cut, we need to clean the cut so we will not get an infection. Our sins are like wounds on our bodies that need to be cleansed by the Blood of Jesus. As the water and Blood flowed from his side when he died on the cross, Jesus cleansed us, he washed us clean so that the infection of sin will not spread throughout our lives. His Blood opens the door to reconciliation with God. "The law requires that nearly everything be cleansed with blood, and without the shedding of blood there is no forgiveness" (Heb 9:22). Isaiah writes: "Though your sins are like scarlet they shall be white as snow; though they be crimson red, they shall be like wool" (Is 1:18).

3. We are sanctified through the Blood. To be sanctified means to be made holy. The Blood of Jesus purifies our lives. It moves over us and through us, purifying us from the effects of our sins. The Blood of Christ transforms us, "for he chose us... to be holy and blameless in his sight" (Eph 1:4). We are to "be holy in all you do; for it is written: 'Be holy, because I am holy'" (1 Pt 1:15, 16). We can fulfill this call through the Blood of Christ which makes us holy.

4. We have union with God through the Blood. To be in union with God is to share in the life of God. We share in that life through our Baptism. In Baptism we are baptized into the death and resurrection of Jesus. When we die to ourselves, when we die to sin, we are united in Jesus Christ.

5. **We have victory over Satan through the Blood.** With Jesus we share in the victory over Satan. "In all these things we are more than conquerors through him who loved us" (Rom 8:37). By the power of his Precious Blood, we have been rescued from the power of darkness. Jesus is the light that shatters the darkness. His powerful light breaks the darkness of sin and suffering. We are a "chosen people, a royal priesthood, a holy nation, a people belonging to God, that you may declare the praises of him who called you out of darkness into his wonderful light" (1 Pt 2:9). In Jesus we have victory over suffering because "by his wounds you have been healed" (1 Pt 2:24).

6. **We have life through the Blood.**[1] Life is not just life here on earth. We share in the promise of everlasting life through Jesus' shed Blood. We receive part of this life now—that is what we call grace (the life of God). We will receive the fullness of this life when we die and meet our God face to face. That is salvation. The growth toward salvation is a process. The beginning of this process is our justification.

The term justification is mentioned fifteen times in the Letter to the Romans, eight times in the Letter to the Galatians, and only two other times in the rest of St. Paul's letters. St. Paul tells us that we are justified through faith in Jesus Christ (Rom 3:22). Justification is the beginning of "*the* process." The process is our sanctification (being made holy, maturation in the Christian life). Salvation is the end of the process. Salvation becomes a fully possessed gift by sanctification. But it all starts with justification. Justification is a holy God's act of making us holy by the Blood of Christ, reconciling the world to relationship with himself (Rom 3:21-27).

St. Paul states that the just person lives by faith (Rom 1:7). He exemplifies this when he speaks of Abraham in chapter four of Romans. It is this faith and the living out of it which brings us peace (Rom 5:1). Justification is a total gift (Rom 3:24). It is an act of God's mercy. But this act also involves active participation and obedience to God's continued goodness. God justified us (Rom 3:30) and God can reject disobedient Christians (Gal 6:7; 5:21). That is why we must continue to live in the grace of our justification. This daily living out of this grace is the grace of sanctification. We depend on the grace merited by Jesus not only to be initially justified but to persevere in his saving grace until the end of life (salvation).

From the beginning to the end of salvation, Jesus is our Savior, but we must willfully cooperate with God's grace. St. James tells us that "faith by itself, if it is not accompanied by action, is dead" (Jas 2:17). By serious sin we can lose the grace of justification. We receive all these great gifts through the shed Blood of Jesus Christ.

Jesus conquered sin and death through the shedding of his Blood. He was obedient to the Father in shedding his Blood for us. Jesus obtained eternal redemption for us by his Blood (Heb 9:12). We were once in slavery, but now we are free, redeemed through the Blood of Christ. Through the sprinkling of the Blood of Jesus, we are able to grow in holiness (1 Pt 1:2). Jesus has made it possible for everybody to share in the blessings of redemption through his Blood (Rv 5:9).

Jesus is both priest and sacrifice, God and temple. He is the priest through whom we have been reconciled, the sacrifice by which we have been reconciled to the Father, the temple in which we have been reconciled and now worship, the God with whom we have been reconciled.[2] Through Jesus Christ we have been reunited with God our loving Father.

It was necessary that Jesus died and shed his Blood for us to be redeemed. In the book of Genesis, we read the story of creation and then the fall of our first parents into sin.

But God, in his great love and mercy, promised a redeemer. He promised that he would send someone to repair the damage that had been done to the world and to the special relationship that human beings experienced with God. St. Paul explains that in the beginning of the world all of creation was in harmony with God. The sin of Adam and Eve destroyed that original harmony. "For just as through the disobedience of the one man the many were made sinners, so also through the obedience of the one man the many will be made righteous" (Rom 5:19). Jesus is that one man whose obedience healed the rift of sin in the world.

The nature of sin is so destructive that the ultimate sacrifice of the Blood of God's only begotten Son was necessary so that we could grow in the holiness of God. Through sin we become guilty; somehow the debt of guilt must be paid. We are delivered from the guilt and debt of sin through Jesus.[3] The Easter Proclamation (the Exultet) from the Easter vigil of Holy Saturday evening proclaims: "For Christ has ransomed us with his blood, and paid for us the price of Adam's sin to our eternal Father."[4]

We share in the blessings of the redemption of Jesus through our faith in this saving Blood. This faith is strengthened by knowledge. Simply put, the greater our knowledge about the power of the shed Blood of Jesus Christ, the more faith we will have.

We need to fully recognize and appreciate the power of this shed Blood. The death and resurrection of Jesus has conquered Satan and his demonic forces (Rv 5:9). Throughout the Book of Revelation, the image used for Christ is a slain lamb. It is through the Blood of the Lamb of God that we receive victory and power over Satan and his demonic forces. Remember, the demons were subject to the seventy-two disciples (Lk 10:17-20). The demons were subject to Paul. The demons were subject to the first Christians. The demons also are subject to us as the present-day followers of the Lord.

To use this power with wisdom and love, we Christians must grow in developing a spiritual life that includes the sacraments of the church, daily prayer, and Scripture reading. In the Sacred Scriptures, we are taught how the Lord dealt with demonic spirits, how to properly use the authority of Jesus in this battle, and how demonic spirits operate.

Though defeated, Satan tries to show that he is strong. Though he will protest, even Satan must admit, "that at the name of Jesus every knee should bow, in heaven and on earth and under the earth, and every tongue confess that Jesus Christ is Lord, to the glory of God the Father" (Phil 2:10-11).

We must never forget that we are more than conquerors through the shed Blood of Jesus Christ (Rom 8:37-39). However, war between nations demonstrates that even though the battle may be won, guerrilla warfare can continue. That is what Satan wages today—guerrilla warfare against Christians. To completely remove an adversary, the land must be cleared of all pockets of resistance. The people of God are called to cleanse the world of Satan and his demons.

We have the power of Jesus Christ with us to do this mighty work. But still, we may feel weak. It is difficult to be rid of the sin in our lives. Even though we believe in the power of the Blood of Christ, we still may experience difficulties. God knows our weaknesses; he knows our struggles. That is why he, in his great love for us, has given us heavenly helpers to assist us in our daily struggle.

FIVE

Our Heavenly Helpers

It was two o'clock in the morning. I had just gotten back from the hospital, giving the sacrament of the sick to an accident victim and comforting the family. I had trouble falling asleep. At about 2:30 that morning the phone rang. It was another emergency at the hospital. I groggily put on my clerical garb and went to the car.

As I drove to the hospital, I could barely keep my eyes open. I stopped at one of the traffic lights. The light turned green and for some reason I did not press the accelerator. I kept my foot on the brake.

Suddenly a car flew past the intersection at about 60 miles per hour. If I had gone through the intersection like I normally do, I would have been broadsided by this speeding car and possibly killed. But something stopped me. I do not remember the rest of the morning, but I know I made it to the hospital. Why didn't I drive through on the green light? Who stopped me?

I believe that my guardian angel was with me and stopped me that night. I have had similar experiences. I cannot count the times that I have been close to having accidents on the freeway. Each time I have been saved, I have thanked my angel for his protection and thanked God for sending me a heavenly guardian as protection.

Most of us have probably had experiences when we were in trouble and somehow it was avoided. Maybe it has happened as we drove on freeways or side streets. Maybe we have been protected while taking a walk. We can't explain these near misses. God in his goodness sends his angels to protect us from harm.

St. John Bosco, whose heroic work with orphan boys and delinquents was opposed, had a special protector. While returning home one night through a bad part of town, St. John Bosco saw a magnificent gray dog of huge size following him. At first he was frightened, but the dog seemed to be friendly. The animal walked by him and accompanied him to his door, then went away. This happened about eight times. He named the dog *Il Grigio*, "the Grey One," in Italian.

One night, on his way home, two shots were fired at him by an assassin. Both shots missed. The assailant then ran toward him. Suddenly Il Grigio appeared and attacked the assailant. Another time two men ambushed him and threw a sack over his head. Again, Il Grigio unexpectedly appeared and rescued him. A third time twelve hired assassins tried to ambush him. Escape seemed impossible, but from nowhere Il Grigio came and rescued him.

Sometimes the dog entered Don Bosco's house, but always for some reason, either to accompany him on a night journey or to prevent him from leaving the house. No amount of animal instinct could explain these unexpected appearances of the dog.

On one of these occasions, when Don Bosco tried to go out, the great gray dog lay across the door and growled in such a menacing way that St. John was forced to remain at home. Shortly afterwards a gentleman arrived to warn him not to leave the home on any consideration, because some evil men were prepared to ambush and kill him.

As long as the opposition to John Bosco's work lasted, Il Grigio never failed to be at his post. When the danger had passed, he was seen no more. Ten years later Don Bosco had to go to the farmhouse of some friends and had been advised that the road was dangerous. "If only I had Il Grigio," he said. At once the great dog appeared at his side, as if he had heard the words. Don Bosco and the dog made it safely to the farmhouse. After the meal, the owner of the farmhouse offered to feed the dog, but he had disappeared.

In 1883, thirty years after the dog's first appearance, he appeared in a different way to guide Don Bosco, who had lost his way.[1] In dog years, the canine protector would have been 210 years old. How is this possible? How do we explain the events surrounding St. Don Bosco and Il Grigio? Most likely this was an angelic intervention to protect one of God's saints.

The purpose of this chapter is to introduce our heavenly helpers: the angels, Mary, and the saints. Later, in chapter nine, I will explain more in depth how we can turn to our heavenly helpers in time of need and how they help us in our spiritual battle.

There are times in our lives when we need another person's help. Maybe the person just listens to our problems. Sometimes he or she may offer solutions to the problems. When I need help in my life, I often ask people to pray for me. Their prayers are a source of strength. The wisdom they share helps me in making difficult decisions. God our Father and Jesus have sent us the Holy Spirit to be a spiritual counselor and guide. God gives us other believers, so we can encourage each other in following his ways. Further, God has given us heavenly helpers. We can call on their aid in time of need as well.

THE ANGELS

As a young boy, I learned the following prayer:

Angel of God, my guardian dear,
to whom God's love entrusts me here.
Ever this day be at my side to light and guard,
to rule and guide. Amen.

When I was afraid at night, all I had to do was say that prayer and gaze upon the picture of the guardian angel that was in my bedroom.

God has given everyone a guardian angel: "Are not all angels ministering spirits sent to serve those who will inherit salvation?" (Heb 1:14). The creation of purely spiritual beings which Sacred Scripture calls "angels" is part of divine revelation.[2]

If someone denies the existence of the angels, then they must radically revise Sacred Scripture and the whole history of salvation.[3] The Fourth Lateran Council in 1215 states: "God at the beginning of time created from nothing both creatures together, the spiritual and the corporeal, that is, the angelic and the earthly, and thus he created human nature as having both since it is made up of spirit and body."[4]

Angels in the Old Testament. To help us understand what the angels do, we must turn to the appearances of the angels in the Scriptures. In the Old Testament, the angels are ministers of the revelations of God. An angel gave Abraham the promise that he would be blessed and his descendants would be as numerous as the stars in the sky. The angel also promised that God would give Abraham a land where his descendants would form a great nation (Gn 22:15-18).

The angels are ministers of the mercy and judgment of God. Hagar was the Egyptian maidservant of Sarah, the wife of Abraham. Sarah had not given Abraham any children, so she gave Hagar to Abraham in order to give him a child. But when Hagar became pregnant, Sarah became jealous. In her jealousy, she mistreated Hagar, so the poor woman fled to the desert with her son, Ishmael. The Lord sent an angel of mercy to Hagar in the desert to guide her (Gn 16). Angels of the Lord also carried out the judgment against Sodom and Gomorrah (Gn 19). The birth of Samson is foretold by an angel (Jgs

13:3). An angel of mercy strengthened Elijah to carry out his prophetic ministry to the people of Israel (1 Kgs 19:5-7).

Shadrach, Meshach, and Abednego were devout Jews. King Nebuchadnezzar of Babylon ordered all the people in his kingdom to worship an idol, an image of gold that he had made. Those who did not bow down before this image were threatened with death by fire in a furnace. These courageous Jewish men did not obey the king's orders, and the king was furious. He again ordered them to worship the image or be thrown into the fiery furnace.

The three Jewish men made a decision to obey their God, placing their faith in the power of the Lord to save them from death. The king had them thrown into the fiery furnace. Amidst the flames, there appeared a fourth man. This was an angel sent by the Lord to protect them from the fire (Dn 3).

Daniel was eminent and trusted in the service of King Darius of the Persians. Other court officials were envious of him. Through tricking the King into signing a particular law that they knew Daniel would disobey, they were able to get Daniel thrown into the lions' den. Even though he remained in the lions' den all night, Daniel was not harmed because "my God sent his angel, and he shut the mouths of the lions" (Dn 6:22).

On another occasion with Daniel, the archangel Gabriel visited him after he had spent time in prayer and fasting to give him a message about the people of Israel. Further, Gabriel mentions another archangel, Michael. Michael had fought off a powerful demon which enabled Gabriel to deliver the message to Daniel.

Angels are even used as agents of God's healing. In the Book of Tobit, the archangel Raphael assists both Tobit and Tobias. The angel protects Tobias on his journey to find a suitable wife from among his kinsfolk and frees his future wife from a demonic spirit. When Tobias returns from his journey, God uses Raphael to heal Tobit's blindness. The name Raphael means: "God heals."[5]

Angels in the New Testament. The New Testament also shows that angels are messengers of God, sent to assist the followers of the Lord. In the Gospels, it is the archangel Gabriel who brings the message to Mary that she is to be the mother of our Lord Jesus Christ (Lk 1:26-38). The name Gabriel means: "my power is God" or "power of God." He is bound especially to the mystery of the Incarnation.[6]

At the birth of Jesus, a choir of angels announces the good news of salvation to the shepherds as they sing: "Glory to God in the highest, and on earth peace to men on whom his favor rests" (Lk 2:14). Just as the angels brought this message to the shepherds, they proclaim the lordship of Jesus to us today.

An angel appears to Joseph in a dream and reveals God's plan. Joseph, in obedience to God's word, takes Mary as his wife (Mt 1:23-24). Joseph, in another dream, receives a message from an angel to flee to Egypt (Mt 2:13). Yet another angel tells Joseph to return to Israel after the death of Herod (Mt 2:19-20). Just as God spoke to Joseph in times of trial and difficulty through these angels, he speaks to us today. Sometimes God will use his revealed Word, the Scriptures. At other times he will use another Christian, but God can also speak his message to us through his angels.

It is interesting that angels ministered to Jesus in times of great need. After a fast of forty days in the desert and enduring the temptations of Satan, "[Jesus] was with the wild animals, and angels attended him" (Mk 1:13). Jesus, on the night before he died, prayed in great anguish of soul while he was in the Garden of Gethsemane that he would be strengthened to do the Father's will. Luke tells us that "an angel from heaven appeared to him and strengthened him" (Lk 22:43). Just as God never abandoned his Son, he will never abandon his people. Help is always there for those who believe.

We need to realize that the angels are not just attractive and beautiful creatures, but powerful allies. They can assist us in our daily battle against Satan and the demonic spirits. Jesus, when he was arrested, said: "Do you think I cannot call on my Father, and he will at once put at my disposal more than twelve legions of angels?" (Mt 26:53). We see St. Michael the archangel and his angels defeat Satan and the demonic spirits in a great battle recounted in the Book of Revelation (Rv 12:7-9).

In the Gospel of Luke, Jesus says: "I saw Satan fall like lightning from heaven" (Lk 10:18). With these words, the Lord affirms that the proclamation of the kingdom of God is always a victory over the Devil. At the same time he also reveals that the building up of the kingdom is continuously exposed to the attacks of the spirit of evil.[7] The Father will send angels to help us in our daily struggles if we ask him for their help.

The angels intercede for us by bringing the prayers of the faithful before the throne of our Father (Rv 5:8). They rejoice over repentant sinners (Lk 15:10). They are our friends—special companions who wish to assist us in our life in God. Part of their work is to help us remain faithful to the Lord so that we may, one day, rejoice with them in the kingdom of heaven.

Guardian angels. The belief that God provides a special angel to guard each of us (called our guardian angel) is demonstrated in the Gospels and the Book of Acts. During the temptation in the desert, Satan quotes Scripture, telling Jesus, "He will command his angels concerning you to guard you carefully" (Lk 4:10). Jesus teaches that each of us has a guardian angel to help us when he says that "their angels in heaven always see the face of my Father in heaven" (Mt 18:10).

In the Acts of the Apostles, King Herod arrested some members of the church. Peter also was apprehended by Herod. The believers prayed that Peter would be freed. God responded to their prayers and sent an angel to free Peter from prison. After Peter was free, he went to the house of Mary, the mother of John. When the servant girl said that Peter was at the door, the believers told her, "It must be his angel" (Acts 12:1-15).

The church confesses her faith in the guardian angels, honoring them with a special feast on October 2. St. Basil writes: "Every one of the faithful has beside him an angel as tutor and pastor, to lead him to life."[8] The Catholic Church also celebrates a special liturgy in honor of the archangels Michael, Gabriel, and Raphael on September 29th.

The angels are gifts from our Father to help us in our daily lives. Psalm 91:11-12 states: "For he will command his angels concerning you to guard you in all your ways; they will lift you up in their hands, so that you will not strike your foot against a stone." God has given us these ministering spirits (Heb 1:14).

But we also have other heavenly helpers. They are Mary and the saints.

MARY: OUR SPIRITUAL MOTHER

In 1991 I went to Medjugorje, in what was then Yugoslavia. It has been reported that Mary has been appearing there to a group of children since 1980. One morning I woke up early and walked to a mountain where Mary had reportedly appeared. As I prayed, I had a very deep experience of the presence of God. When I prayed the rosary on that mountain, I felt the presence of Mary as well.

Then I knew in my heart that Mary was present in that place. Her presence was a protection for the people of that little town and the pilgrims who came. But I also realized that someone else was present. Satan and his demons were there as well, waiting for an opportunity to inhibit the grace of God that was being poured out on the people.

Mary has reportedly appeared in various places throughout the years. God has sent Mary as a messenger to his faithful people. The message of Mary in her apparitions is usually that we need to repent of our sins and pray more. She calls us to a new conversion of the heart. She is our advocate and special helper in the spiritual battle.

The most famous set of Marian apparitions occurred in Fatima, Portugal. They have been declared genuine by the church, although Catholics are not required to believe in them since they are considered a private revelation. On May 13, 1917, she appeared to three children: Lucia, Jacinta, and Francisco. There were six apparitions from May to October 13. A seventh apparition was given only to Lucia in 1921. The October apparition was the occasion of a great miracle—the miracle of the sun, where the sun appeared to plummet to the earth, spin, and give off a multi-colored light. The site of Fatima has become a world-famous place of pilgrimage.

Who is this powerful messenger and instrument of God? She is the mother of Jesus Christ and dwells now in heaven. From heaven she intercedes for us, her spiritual children. Mary has a precise place in the plan of salvation. We can only understand Mary's place in salvation history through understanding the mystery of Jesus Christ. When Mary is honored, her Son is duly acknowledged, loved, and glorified, and his commandments are observed.[9]

Because she is the mother of Jesus, Mary has a special place in spiritual warfare as well. Genesis 3:15 states: "I will put enmity between you and the woman, and between your offspring and hers; he will crush your head, and you will strike his heel." Mary as the New Eve is the woman referred to in this passage. Her obedience was the opposite of Eve's disobedience in the Garden of Eden. Eve, the mother of the human race, was instrumental in the fall from grace of humanity. Mary, the New Eve, is instrumental in the salvation of the human race by agreeing to be the mother of Jesus. If we are able to grasp the significance of her role in crushing Satan, then we can better grasp the grandeur of God's plan.

In the Book of Revelation we have a description of the war in the heavens (Rv 12:7-9). Satan was hurled down to the earth, and was "enraged at the woman and went off to make war against the rest of the offspring—those who obey God's commandments and hold to the testimony of Jesus" (Rv 12:17). The woman is the church and secondarily Mary, as the model of the church. Christians are her offspring. This is consistent with what Jesus said on the cross to Mary and the beloved disciple, John, "Dear woman, here is your son... Here is your mother" (Jn 19:26-27). In this declaration, Jesus united us to his mother since the apostle John stands for all of the disciples of Jesus.

Jesus, while he was dying on the cross, gave his Mother to us. Consider what this means: We have a spiritual mother to care for us. Through the power of the Holy Spirit she conceived Jesus. Through the power of Jesus and with the special anointing of the Holy Spirit, Mary is commissioned to be the Mother of all Christians. One of the titles of Mary is Help of Christians. She is our intercessor who loves us with the tenderness of a mother. In becoming the human mother of the Son of God, in whom we are one, sole, living being for all eternity, Mary contracted a unique solidarity with all humanity. She was called to be mother of all.[10]

Mary is Jesus' gift to us. Her love is:

> the instrument of God's own maternal love, which was only implicit in the biblical term "Father" but is clearly and beautifully mediated in a unique way through Mary. She is not a metaphorical appendage but a revelation in person of the maternal face of God.... Her maternal love is first of all God's love for us. If, in the historical tradition that has come

down to us, God has chosen to be known as *Abba* and to allow the overflowing maternal dimension of that love to be mediated through Mary, it would seem most fruitful to follow the revealed pattern and to allow God to exercise his mothering of us through her rather than trying to introject a functional motherhood or title "Mother" into the Godhead, however theoretically valid that might be.[11]

God did not leave us a title to demonstrate his motherly love for us. He gave us a living symbol, a human person, a human mother. That is why Mary is so special to all believers. God chose her to reveal his motherly love for each of us. That is why Mary is called our spiritual mother. Just as children have a natural love for their mothers, so Christians have a natural love for Mary, their spiritual mother.

The Father planned that Jesus would be born of a woman by the power of the Holy Spirit. In this plan Jesus would save men and women from sin by lowering himself below the angels and becoming man. In doing so, Lucifer (Satan) would thus be lower than the woman and her offspring.[12] He could not stand this humiliation and rebelled, saying, "I will not serve!"

Mary, in her response to the angel Gabriel's greeting, says, "I am the Lord's servant" (Lk 1:38). This is the opposite of Satan's "I will not serve." She shows us that the life of a Christian is praise, humility, service, and obedience to God.

Mary is the instrument chosen by God to crush Satan. It is her flesh—the Word made flesh, and his body, the church, that crushes Satan.[13] The uniqueness of Mary's role in spiritual warfare is that she is part of God's redemptive plan. The Lord chose a human being, a woman, someone totally human, to be an instrument of his victory over Satan.[14] Mary's continuing role in spiritual warfare is to be a model of virtue for us and an intercessor for us as our spiritual mother. Her goal is to bring us into the heart of Jesus, our Lord and her Son.

To venerate Mary correctly means to acknowledge her Son, for she is the Mother of God. To love her means to love Jesus, for she is his mother. To ask for the intercession of Our Lady means not to substitute her for Christ, but to glorify her Son who desires us to have loving confidence in his saints, especially in his mother.[15]

Mary is introduced into the mystery of Christ through the Annunciation where she is asked to be the mother of the Savior. It is in this passage of Scripture that we realize Mary received a special grace from God. This gift is the Immaculate Conception.

The doctrine of the Immaculate Conception states that Mary, in the first instant of her conception was, by a singular grace and privilege of Almighty God in view of the merits of Jesus Christ, the Savior of the human race, preserved from all stain of original sin. The Immaculate Conception does not refer to the conception of Jesus Christ. The Immaculate Conception does not mean that Mary was conceived "by the power of the Holy Spirit" in the same way that Jesus was. The Immaculate Conception means that Mary, whose conception was brought about in the normal human way, was conceived in the womb of her mother without original sin.

In order to understand this dogma of the Catholic Church, one must study the angel's greeting to Mary in the Gospel of Luke. In Luke 1:28 the angel says, "Greetings, you who are highly favored!" The Greek word for highly favored is *kecharitomene*. According to the renowned Mariologist René Laurentin, the Greek word *kecharitomene* means much more than highly favored. He states that "the word both theologically and philologically indicates a transformation of the subject." Therefore, Mary is transformed by this favor or grace. Since the Greek word indicates a perfection of grace, this transforming grace is a permanent grace.[16]

Because this grace is a perfection of grace, Mary enjoyed this grace throughout her whole life, from the moment of her conception. Mary received this special divine favor through the merits of Jesus Christ, applied to her before he was even conceived in her womb. Mary required a Savior. Like all of us, her nature would have been subject to original sin. But through the intervention of Almighty God, through whom all things are possible, she was preserved from original sin. She was redeemed by the grace of Christ in a special way, by anticipation.[17]

Because of this grace, Mary occupies a special place in God's kingdom. One of her titles is Mediatrix of All Graces. This does not mean that she is Mediator. Christ alone is the perfect Mediator between God and humanity. Through his death he reconciled the world to the Father. However, nothing hinders others from being called mediators. After all, we mediate for others when we pray to God on their behalf.[18] And Mary does this in a special way because of her role in our salvation.

All our prayers for one another are founded upon the supreme mediation of Jesus Christ. All our efforts are completely dependent on him. Mary's prayers as a mediatrix for us are dependent upon her Son.

The church celebrates different feasts of Mary throughout the year to remind us of her special role in salvation. The church also promotes special prayers (devotions) to Mary, the most prominent being the rosary. These prayers are a method of asking for her intercession to Jesus for our needs. The bishops of the Church encourage us to pray to Mary for her assistance because Marian devotions can bring us closer to Jesus.[19]

THE SAINTS: OUR INTERCESSORS IN HEAVEN

Near Albuquerque, New Mexico, there is a church that has a special staircase. The church had been built, but there was not enough money to build the staircase that was to go from the ground floor to the choir loft. The priest and sisters of the parish prayed that a carpenter would come and build the staircase for free since there was not enough money to pay for the materials and labor to build it.

One day a young man came to the door of the church and offered to build it for them. The wood that he used was an expensive type that came from another part of New Mexico. And he did not use any screws or nails to build the staircase. Further, the staircase is a spiral one and has no visible means of suport. Who built this miraculous staircase? Could it be that the prayers of the priest and sisters for a carpenter reached the ears of St. Joseph, a carpenter and the husband of Mary?

The Catholic Church has the tradition of honoring people as saints who have followed the call of God in an exemplary way. The Catholic Church states that these men and women are definitely in heaven, yet never in its history has it worshiped the saints as if they were God.

The word "worship" comes from the Old English *weorthscipe*, which means the condition of being worthy of honor, respect, or dignity. In the older sense of the word, "to worship" means to give someone honor, whether that person be a government official or God. The highest worship or highest honor is given to God alone. The honor given to saints is different from that given to God. In some older Catholic writings one finds the term "worship of the saints." The word "worship" is being used in its original sense, that of giving honor. Today the word "worship" has the connotation of adoration. That is why today it is improper to use the term "worship" in referring to Mary and the saints. The proper term is "veneration" or "honor." For example, we venerate Mary because she is the mother of Jesus. This honor does not make her equal to God, but she does have a special place in heaven because of her obedience to the will of God. As we have seen, in being the mother of Jesus she is also our spiritual mother.

To show honor to someone is common. In the United States a justice of a court is addressed as "Your Honor." In marriage vows one promises to "love and honor." People who have died for their country are honored, and people are honored for heroic deeds. Our government leaders are honored because of the office they hold. In Scripture one reads: "Honor your father and your mother" (Ex 20:12). There is nothing wrong with giving people honor whether they be living or deceased, especially if the deceased are before the throne of God praising him.

In the Scriptures, angels are honored (venerated). Joshua honors an angel who is the captain of the host of the Lord. "Now when Joshua was near Jericho, he looked up and saw a man standing in front of him with a drawn sword in his hand. Joshua went up to him and asked, 'Are you for us or for our enemies?' 'Neither,' he replied, 'but as commander of the army of the Lord I have now come.' Then Joshua fell facedown to the ground in reverence, and asked him, 'What message does my Lord have for his servant?'" (Jos 5:13-14).

The prophet Daniel also honors an angel who brings him a message: "While I, Daniel, was watching the vision and trying to understand it, there before me stood one who looked like a man. And I heard a man's voice from the Ulai calling, 'Gabriel, tell this man the meaning of the vision.' As he came near the place where I was standing, I was terrified and fell prostrate" (Dn 8:15-17).

In Tobit one reads: "'I am Raphael, one of the seven holy angels who present the prayers of the saints and enter into the presence of the glory of the Holy One.' They were both alarmed; and they fell upon their faces, for they were afraid. But he said to them, 'Do not be afraid; you will be safe. But praise God forever. For I did not come as a favor on my part, but by the will of our God. Therefore praise him forever'" (Tb 12:15-18).

As with the angels, the saints are united with God. They are before the throne of God because they see him as he is. "Dear friends, now we are children of God, and what we will be has not yet been made known. But we know that when he appears, we shall be like him, for we shall see him as he is" (1 Jn 3:2).

When a family member dies, the family usually keeps pictures or mementos of him or her. These mementos help to remind us of the person we miss. As people look upon their loved one's likeness, they remember moments they shared, how the person lived, and his or her *dedication* to God. The same is true with the saints. They are our brothers and sisters, members of the family of God who are now in heaven.

Pictures and statues in Catholic churches are not gods, then, but simply representations of Jesus, Mary, and the saints to remind us of their dedication to the one, true God. Since we are the family of God, they are like mementos to remind us of Jesus and the saints who have gone before us. "The fact that someone kneels before a statue to pray does not mean that he is praying to the statue, just as the fact that one kneels with a Bible in his hands—as fundamentalists at times do—does not mean that he or she is worshiping the Bible. Statues or paintings or other artistic devices are used to recall to the mind of the person the thing depicted. Just as it is easier to remember one's mother by looking at her photograph, so it is easier to recall the lives of the saints, and thus be edified by their examples, by looking at representations of them."[20]

Saints and their intercession for us. Death does not mean that someone is no longer alive. Death means that the person is no longer here on this earth and thus can no longer be seen. Those who have died and are in heaven are alive to God. Jesus had to remind the Sadduccees of this. "Have you not read in the book of Moses, in the account of the bush, how God said to him, 'I am the God of Abraham, the God of Isaac, and the

God of Jacob'? He is not the God of the dead, but of the living" (Mk 12:26-27). The saints are in heaven, before the throne of God. In the account of the transfiguration Moses and Elijah appeared in glory and spoke with Jesus. When Peter saw this he said, "Master, it is good for us to be here. Let us put up three shelters—one for you, one for Moses and one for Elijah" (Lk 9:28-34). In this passage the intent of the shelters was to honor Jesus, Moses, and Elijah.

Just as people on earth pray for one another, so the saints in heaven, who are members of a person's spiritual family, pray for the people of God still on earth. At death people are not cut off from one another. There is a different bond, a spiritual bond in the Lord. This is what the Catholic Church calls the communion of saints.

This term, which is also called the mystical body of Christ, expresses the common bond that is shared by those who are in communion with God. The understanding of this term comes from the Gospel of John: "I am the vine; you are the branches. If a man remains in me and I in him, he will bear much fruit; apart from me you can do nothing" (Jn 15:5). Those connected to Christ are also connected to one another. Those who have died and are in heaven are still connected to Christ. Therefore, they remain related to the people of God on earth.[21]

This relationship also is expressed by Paul in 1 Corinthians 12:12-27. In this passage Paul explains that the people of God are united, just as the body is united. If one part is suffering, all the members suffer with it. If one member is honored, all are honored with it. The people of God share a mystical union with one another through Jesus Christ. "Just as each of us has one body with many members, and these members do not all have the same function, so in Christ we who are many form one body, and each member belongs to all the others" (Rom 12:4-5).

A natural, even a necessary, inference from this teaching is intercessory prayer. Paul asks: "I urge you, brothers, by our

Lord Jesus Christ and by the love of the Spirit, to join me in my struggle by praying to God for me" (Rom 15:30). Hebrews 13:18 encourages the faithful to pray for the leadership of the church.

The saints are branches of the vine of Jesus Christ in heaven. The followers of God on earth, the branches of the vine on earth, are encouraged to intercede for one another. Therefore, the saints, who are still members of the vine, can intercede for the followers of God on earth as well. The saints in heaven pray for the saints of God on earth.

The angels and saints also can place the prayers of the faithful before the throne of God. As the angel told Tobit, "And so, when you and your daughter-in-law Sarah prayed, I brought a reminder of your prayer before the Holy One; and when you buried the dead, I was likewise present with you" (Tb 12:12).

People can honor a saint by praying to him or her, which means asking for that saint's intercession, and not worshipping the saint. This is similar to asking a friend here on earth to pray for one's needs. When a person asks for a saint's intercession, the saint brings the intentions of this person to God. "And when he had taken it [the scroll], the four living creatures and the twenty-four elders fell down before the Lamb. Each one had a harp and they were holding golden bowls full of incense, which are the prayers of the saints" (Rv 5:8). And again, "Another angel, who had a golden censer, came and stood at the altar. He was given much incense to offer, with the prayers of all the saints, on the golden altar before the throne. The smoke of the incense, together with the prayers of the saints, went up before God from the angel's hand" (Rv 8:3-4).

Jesus himself alludes to the possibility of intercessory prayer. In Luke 16:19-31 in the parable of the rich man and Lazarus, the rich man who has been condemned to hell is seeking help from Lazarus. He first asks for personal comfort. Then he asks for Lazarus to help his family so that they will follow God. This asking for assistance is a type of prayer, that is, seeking the intercession of Lazarus.

Our heavenly helpers—the angels, Mary, and the saints—have a valid role in heaven as intercessors on our behalf. We are to honor the angels as spirits created by God to assist us in our lives. We are to honor Mary and the saints as holy men and women who have gone before us. But the power of their intercession is completely dependent upon the power of God.

We do need their prayers and their assistance as members of our spiritual family, for the spiritual battle takes place in every part of our lives, both in our hearts and minds and when faced with the temptations of the world, the flesh, and the Devil. Paul says: "For our struggle is not against flesh and blood, but against the rulers, against the authorities, against the powers of this dark world and against the spiritual forces of evil in the heavenly realms" (Eph 6:12).

PART TWO:

The Battleground

The Battle Within

Why me, O Lord? Why is this happening to me? I pray, and I go to Mass. I go to confession regularly, and I read the Bible. Why don't you hear my prayers? I feel so alone. Where can I turn for help in my life? The weight is too much to bear. I feel that I cannot go on with this pain in my life. "I am feeble and utterly crushed; I groan in anguish of heart" (Ps 38:8). Why, Lord, why are you allowing this to happen to your faithful one? "My life is consumed by anguish.... But I trust in you, O Lord" (Ps 31:10, 14).

I believe that everyone who has walked the path of God has felt this way sometime in life. It is not easy to follow the ways of God. In the beginning of our relationship with God, there will be peace and joy, but eventually we will be faced with periods of disillusionment and pain. We may feel that we are in darkness, that there is no hope or consolation in our lives. Our faith is put to the supreme test. This is the spiritual battle at its fiercest moment—feeling totally abandoned by God.

SPIRITUAL WARFARE

As we have seen, we are involved in spiritual warfare (Eph 6:12). This warfare began with the revolt of Satan and the demonic spirits. The consequences of their revolt was that they were cast out of heaven down to earth where "the devil prowls around like a roaring lion looking for someone to devour" (1 Pt 5:8).

The spiritual battle is both direct and indirect. Satan directly attacks us through temptation and oppression. Temptation is having an inclination to disobey the will of God. When we do this we place our will above the will of God. Picture yourself within a group of friends. You are having a good time, talking about the things that have happened that day or over the past week. As you talk, someone asks, "Did you hear that John and Mary are getting a divorce?" One of your friends replies, "Yes, I never thought that their marriage would last. They fight so much with each other. Last week I heard that Mary accused John of having an extramarital affair." As you listen, you begin to agree with others. And you start to add a couple of things that you know about John and Mary.

Do you realize what has just happened in this discourse. A nice, friendly conversation has turned into *gossip*. All of us are guilty of this, yet we don't even realize what we are doing most of the time. When we partake in gossip, we are destroying a person's character and reputation. Remember—we are cautioned "not [to] let any unwholesome talk come out of your mouths, but only what is helpful for building others up according to their needs, that it may benefit those who listen" (Eph 4:29).

In this situation, Satan has enticed you to sin. His desire is to ensnare us through his lies and empty promises. You might have felt good while gossiping about John and Mary, but would you want people to talk about you or the problems in your marriage in the same way?

Further, he attacks us indirectly through his influence over the worldly affairs because "the whole world is under the control of the evil one" (1 Jn 5:19). For example, the predominant media message today is, "If it feels good, do it." The leading cause of fatal automobile accidents is alcoholism, yet how many commercials do we have on television that glorify drinking alcohol? How many cases of spousal abuse are related to alcohol? But we are told by the media that in order to feel good, in order to have fun, we need to drink alcohol. We are indoctrinated with messages like this from the media every day—messages that will lead us into sin if we are not careful.

Satan is deceitful, cunning, and intelligent. He attacks us in the weakest area of our lives. But we must remember: our adversary suffers a serious disadvantage: he is not omniscient, omnipotent, or omnipresent like our God.[1]

THE CHRISTIAN'S STRUGGLE

Even though we are baptized and freed from original sin, we still experience a struggle in trying to follow God's commands. St. Paul says "to put off your old self, which is being corrupted by its deceitful desires; to be made new in the attitude of your minds; and to put on the new self, created to be like God in true righteousness and holiness" (Eph 4:22-24). There is a constant battle within us; the primary focus of this battle is in our minds.

We are to live with the mind of Christ, but part of us refuses to serve our God. Our minds are assailed by so many images from movies, television shows, and magazines that glorify a non-Christian worldview. Over time we can be swayed by this onslaught of immoral values. We must also face our peers who are not following God's word and who ridicule our beliefs and morality. Are we strong enough to stand against this onslaught? Do we have enough integrity to proclaim a Christian message to a non-Christian in a hostile world? Are we committed enough to live our faith? This is the daily struggle of the Christian life.

Paul described this struggle in his letter to the Romans:

I do not understand what I do. For what I want to do I do
not do, but what I hate I do. And if I do what I do not want
to do, I agree that the law is good. As it is, it is no longer I
myself who do it, but it is sin living in me. I know that nothing good lives in me, that is, in my sinful nature. For I have
the desire to do what is good, but I cannot carry it out. For
what I do is not the good I want to do; no, the evil I do not
want to do—this I keep on doing. Now if I do what I do not
want to do, it is no longer I who do it, but it is sin living in
me that does it.

So I find this law at work: When I want to do good, evil is
right there with me. For in my inner being I delight in God's
law; but I see another law at work in the members of my
body, waging war against the law of my mind and making
me a prisoner of the law of sin at work within my members.
What a wretched man I am! Who will rescue me from this
body of death? Thanks be to God—through Jesus Christ our
Lord!

So then, I myself in my mind am a slave to God's law, but
in the sinful nature a slave to the law of sin. Romans 7:15-25

We must never underestimate the power of sin. We cannot
fight sin on our own strength. We need the power of Jesus
Christ in our lives to fight this battle. Satan is a crafty tempter,
and we ourselves have an amazing ability to make excuses. We
are ultimately responsible for our actions. The Devil does not
make us sin. We choose sin. That is why it is so difficult to
understand our propensity to sin. We know what we should do,
but we do not always do it.

For Paul, the "law at work within our bodies" is the sinful
tendency deep within us. This is everything within us that
causes us to disobey the commandments of God. We cannot

stand up to sin alone. We need to unite ourselves to the power of the Blood of Jesus Christ to conquer the sin in our lives.

SIN AGAINST OURSELVES

We sin against ourselves when we do not accept our human dignity. Our dignity is founded on Jesus Christ. In the Second Eucharistic Prayer of the Mass, the priest thanks God because he has made us worthy to be his servants. The source of our dignity is God. He has done this for us, we did not do it on our own. "The Spirit himself testifies with our spirit that we are God's children" (Rom 8:16). All our joy is based upon this special family relationship that we have with God.

But Satan tries to rob us of this joy. He tells us that we are unloved. He tells us that we are not really God's children. He tells us that we are unforgivable. When we buy the lie of Satan, we are robbed of our joy. We then believe that we are not worthy to be God's servants. We begin to wallow in the pit of depression and low self-esteem.

Low self-esteem is the root of many problems that people experience today. Low self-esteem has its roots in unhealthy shame. Shame is different from guilt. Guilt says that I did something wrong. Shame says I *am* wrong. Shame is the root of many psychological problems. Shame is a primary component of addictive behavior.

In examining shame it is important to remember that some shame is important for individual growth. The good shame helps us to form proper boundaries.

The central task of the life-work can be construed as one of evolving a uniquely personal identity that gives inherent meaning to one's life, provides direction and purpose to one's work, and enables one's *self* to retain a sense of inner worth and valuing in the face of all those vicissitudes of life with which we must contend, not the least of which are anxiety, suffering, and the lack of absolute control over our own lives.... Some experiencing of defeat, failure, or rejection is inescapable in life. It is this fundamental reality which makes of shame a universal, inevitable occurrence as well as a potential obstacle in the development of a secure, self-affirming identity. And, yet, some degree of shame is necessary precisely in order for identity even to evolve.[2]

Some shame is necessary for our personal growth. It is the toxic (unhealthy) shame[3] that must be dealt with in our lives if we are to grow into healthy integration. Unhealthy shame many times comes to us through our family background. The shame is strengthened through relationships in school settings, work, or one's peer group. Shame usually follows a dominance hierarchy, from the stronger to the weaker.[4] The shame does not begin within us. It comes from outside ourselves.

This is what happens: our parents and family members taught us that we have limitations. This is the basis of healthy shame. But sometimes our caretakers do or say things that inflict a deep wound in us. If this consistently happens, we begin to form a sense that we are flawed. Remember, to a child a parent can do no wrong. A child believes that if there is a problem in a family he or she is the reason for the problem.

Achieving a secure identity is essential for individuals in order to accomplish the natural sequence of developmental tasks so necessary to becoming a fully separate person. When sufficient shame generates early in life through developmental failures, the growth process is disrupted, perhaps even blocked, and a secure, self-affirming identity fails to emerge.... The important link between shame internalization and the formation of a shame-based identity lies in a process by which the self within the growing person begins to actively *disown* parts of itself, thereby creating splits within the self.[5]

We can be shamed in many ways in our families. Shame can come from verbal abuse, physical abuse, sexual abuse, abandonment, overprotective parents, and emotional abuse. When the interpersonal bridge, a vehicle that facilitates mutual understanding and growth between the parents and child, is broken the result is shame.[6] The key to becoming free of toxic, unhealthy shame is to restore the interpersonal bridge that was broken in childhood. For this to happen the shame needs to be brought to the conscious level. As long as shame remains internalized and autonomous, real change is prevented.[7] And since unhealthy shame leads to disowning of parts of the self (and splits off of the real self) being free of unhealthy shame will lead to personal integration.

The unresolved shame issues of parents are passed on to their children. This shame cycle is passed on through the generations until it is broken. It can be broken through psychological counseling or prayer therapy. In prayer therapy, the roots of the shame are discovered through counseling and are brought to Jesus in prayer. The power of the Blood of Christ can then break the chains of shame.

When we let go of the shame, we are transformed. We put aside the previous low self-esteem and accept our God-given dignity as children that he loves unconditionally. Sometimes we want to accept that dignity on our own terms. Christians are challenged to accept righteousness on God's terms—the saving power of the Blood of Jesus Christ. Try as we might, we cannot earn it.

Are we living with hidden secrets—hidden sins, a sense of unworthiness, or toxic shame? The remedy is to invite the power of Christ's Blood to renew every part of our lives. If you are dealing with toxic shame in your life, pray Romans 8:1. But before you read this passage pray: *Heavenly Father, I want to know, at the very depth of my being, the power of the shed Blood of Jesus Christ for me. I want to believe that I am worth the shedding of the Blood of Christ. Holy Spirit, reveal this passage of Scripture to me, that I may once and for all know the power of the Blood of Christ. Help me to let go of my self-condemnation, my toxic shame.* Then open your Bible to Romans 8:1 and read it out loud. Let the truth of God's Word begin to take root deep within your heart.

UNDERSTANDING TEMPTATION

There are two kinds of wisdom that we can live by. The wisdom of God is pure, peace-loving, considerate, submissive, full of mercy and good fruit, impartial and sincere. The other wisdom harbors bitter envy and selfish ambition. This wisdom is earthly, unspiritual, and from the Devil (Jas 3:14-17). The choice is ours. We can choose life or death.

> The acts of the sinful nature are obvious: sexual immorality, impurity and debauchery; idolatry and witchcraft; hatred, discord, jealousy, fits of rage, selfish ambition, dissensions, factions and envy; drunkenness, orgies, and the like. I warn you, as I did before, that those who live like this will not inherit the kingdom of God.
>
> But the fruit of the Spirit is love, joy, peace, patience, kindness, goodness, faithfulness, gentleness and self-control.
>
> **Galatians 5:19-23**

Satan is the great tempter. He wishes to draw us away from God. But remember, temptation is not sin. Jesus was tempted in the desert, but he did not sin. The temptation is not wrong in itself. It is the giving in to the temptation that is sinful. We must also remember that we will never be tempted beyond our strength to resist the temptation. The grace of God is always there for us to resist the sin if we turn to him. We cannot escape responsibility for our actions.

In using temptation, Satan tries to attack our minds and our emotions (internal). He also attacks us though the world around us. Two primary weapons that Satan uses in his arsenal to attack us internally are the undermining of our conscience and sin-based oppression.[8]

UNDERMINING OF OUR CONSCIENCE

If we get a deep cut on our arm, we need proper medical attention. If we do not clean the cut, we may get an infection. If the infection is not properly treated, the infection could spread and become serious, even resulting in the amputation of our arm. If the arm is not amputated, the infection will spread throughout our whole body and even kill us. In a similar way, our conscience can be infected through the belief system of the world.

Because of modern psychology, there is a tendency to rationalize sinful behavior. We make excuses for the wrong things that we do. Some schools of psychology try to convince us that if we were treated better when we were children, we would not act in this or that way today. For example, sinful actions such as getting drunk, sexual promiscuity, foul language, and lying are explained away by saying, "I can't help it." We think it's too difficult or we aren't strong enough to resist. So we give up. While psychology can be an aid to growth in holiness, psychology also can hinder growth in holiness. Some schools of psychology, especially the Rogerian school, have had damaging effects on religious commitment in the church.

In order to avoid a direct confrontation with the Gospel, those who think of themselves as practicing Christians, when faced with a conflict between self-fulfillment and the higher order of Christian values, will generally adopt the rationalization: "I can't do it." It sounds better than saying, "I won't do it." And since psychology has revealed many areas of real but relative psychological impossibility, the rationalization is a comfortable and handy one.[9]

Psychology can only be a help to a person's spiritual growth when it is properly and cautiously used. The Christian must always remember that the goal of his or her life is growth in holiness as a means of drawing closer to God. The Lord said: "Be holy, because I am holy" (1 Pt 1:16).

Our conscience is also undermined by the media. We only need to look at the morality that is projected on our televisions and movie screens to realize that biblical values are under attack. Wanton lust, violence, and graft are projected as desirable lifestyles.

The prevailing secularization of our country promotes a new god—the human being. God is declared as dead. Morality is reduced to, "If it feels good, do it." If I am in love, I do not need to be married in order to have a sexual relationship. All I need is a condom, and all will be well. I won't get AIDS.

Our Christian churches need to stand up and proclaim the message of the Bible to an immoral world. The Christian churches can no longer compromise their values and teachings.

If we have a compromised conscience, we need to honestly admit it and take the following steps to change:

1. Realize the anti-Christian values of the society in which you live. Take responsibility for how you have encouraged those values in your own life, in your home, and in your church.

2. Repent. A Catholic needs to go to confession to receive God's forgiveness and reconciliation for ways in which he or she has compromised gospel values.

3. Return to prayer. Seek wisdom by reflecting on God's word (especially Mt 5-7; Eph 4:17; 6:9; and Ex 20:1-17). Learn the teachings of the church, especially in the area of living a moral life.

SIN-BASED OPPRESSION

In our lives we can develop a sinful tendency. Some sinful tendencies develop into psychological addictions and become a pattern of repeated sin. We become addicts when we rely on a substance to make us feel good. An addict is anyone who has a pathological relationship with any mood-altering experience that has life damaging consequences.

We can be addicted to alcohol, drugs, food, anger, rage, sex, spending, gambling, or anything that fulfills the above definition. If the addictive cycle is not stopped, these addictions will become ingrained in our lives. They become areas of severe oppression. But they are based not only on a psychological addictive process but also on a pattern of sin. Remember that the root of all addictions is shame. The shame and its resulting addiction is like a dark cloud that hovers over our lives, oppressing us. We must invite the power of Jesus Christ into these dark areas for God "has rescued us from the dominion of darkness and brought us into the kingdom of the Son he loves, in whom we have redemption, the forgiveness of sins" (Col 1:13-14). These strongholds of darkness draw their power from two areas. One can be an attack from Satan himself. The other power source of this sinful tendency is unresolved pain in our lives.

For example, if a woman was physically abused while she was

growing up, she may have a tendency toward rage and anger. Only when the issue of abuse is properly dealt with, is it possible to be free of the seething rage inside. A combination of psychological counseling and prayer for inner healing can help a person be free of this rage.

The counseling helps to get to the root of the problem. In inner healing prayer, we invite Jesus to heal the deep-seated hurt. When the inner pain is completely healed, the person is usually free from that compulsion. The more freedom from pain that we have, the more able we are to make a free decision to follow the commands of God.

Everyone is in need of inner healing. All of us have unresolved pain in our lives. A good way of dealing with this pain is to seek forgiveness. When we can forgive those who hurt us, we can let go of the pain and live in peace. Sometimes this is easy to do. At other times it is very difficult. When I have a difficulty in forgiving others, I try to picture myself at the foot of the cross. As Jesus says, "Father forgive them, for they do not know what they are doing," I ask for the grace to receive his forgiveness into my heart.

Then I picture the people I need to forgive kneeling down beside me at the foot of the cross. I imagine Jesus speaking to them those same words of forgiveness. Then I allow Jesus to ask me to forgive them; I pray for the grace to forgive. If I feel that I still cannot forgive someone at this time, I ask Jesus to forgive him or her for me until I can forgive. After that I ask Jesus, by the power of his five wounds on the cross, to heal any pain that I experienced from the relationship.

Along with such deep-seated internal wounds from the past, we receive characteristics from our parents. For example, the color of our eyes and hair comes from the genetic makeup of our parents. Our body frame and other physical characteristics come from our parents. Our intellectual capabilities and our temperament are also based upon our generational heritage.

Since our physical, intellectual, and emotional characteristics come from our heritage, is it possible that we also receive spiritual characteristics from previous generations in our family? Yes, I believe that we do. We receive both positive (prayer-filled) and negative (sin-based) tendencies from our heritage.

Exodus 20:5-6 states: "I, the Lord your God, am a jealous God, punishing the children for the sin of the fathers to the third and fourth generation of those who hate me, but showing love to a thousand [generations] of those who love me and keep my commandments." There can be a sinful strain in our families. For example, have you known families in which everyone has a bad temper? Or have you known families that have predisposition to alcoholism? Or families in which many members tend to experience adulterous relationships or divorce? There are sinful tendencies that can be passed down through the generations.

The following prayer can help break generational sinful tendencies (pray in the name of your family). Before praying this prayer, ask the Holy Spirit to reveal specific sinful patterns of your family.

O Lord, the great and awesome God,
who keeps his covenant of love with all who love him and obey his
commands, we have sinned and done wrong. We have been
wicked and have rebelled; we have turned away from your com-
mands and laws... O Lord, we and... our fathers and mothers
are covered with shame because we have sinned against you.

The Lord our God is merciful and forgiving, even though we
have rebelled against him; we have not obeyed the Lord our God
or kept the laws he gave us.... We have not sought the favor of
the Lord our God by turning from our sins and giving atten-
tion to your truth.... We have sinned, we have done wrong....

Now, our God, hear the prayers and petitions of your ser-
vant. For your sake, O Lord, look with favor on your desolate

sanctuary. Give ear, O God, and hear; open your eyes and see the desolation of the city that bears your name. We do not make requests of you because we are righteous, but because of your great mercy. O Lord, listen! O Lord, forgive! (adapted from Dn 9:4-19).

Forgive our family its past sins and transgressions. Come, Lord Jesus, and heal us. I ask you, Jesus, to purify the moment of my conception through the power of your cross and shed Blood. Remove all negative traits that were passed on through my conception and release all the positive, life-giving traits from my family heritage.

I ask permission from you, Lord, to stand in for my ancestors and in their name I forgive all those who have hurt them in their lives. (When we pray in this way we are representing the generations of our families. In civil law, the lawyer is a representative for his client. He speaks for his client. When there is a dispute between countries, the leaders speak on behalf of the people of that country. If country 'A' has unjustly attacked country 'B,' the leader of country 'A' can stand in the name of the citizens of his country and ask forgiveness of country 'B.' The leader of country 'B' can stand in the name of the citizens of country 'B' and forgive country 'A.' The same is true with our ancestors. As representatives of them, like leaders of countries, we can forgive and ask forgiveness.) *Let the love of the Holy Spirit flow through these relationships, bringing them healing. In their name, I also ask forgiveness of all those whom my ancestors hurt. Again, Lord, send your Holy Spirit to heal these relationships.*

Pour forth the waters of my Baptism over the generations of my family to heal the pain and confusion of my ancestors that caused sinful patterns. In the name of Jesus Christ and by the power of his precious Blood, I break all curses, hexes, seals, spells and consequences of evil that may have entered my family. (In order to discern if there has been a curse or hex placed upon one's family, we need the wisdom of prayer, the wisdom of psychology, and common sense. Sometimes people sensationalize the demonic. We need to have a balanced approach to this problem. A very important gift in discerning if there is a spiritual problem like a curse or a hex is the gift of discernment of spirits. This is covered in detail in chapter eight.) *I thank you and I praise you for setting me and my family free of these generational bondages* (you can mention specific sinful patterns). *Send your Holy Spirit to fill us with your peace and love. May we now be healed and be the family that you have called us to be. I ask this in the name of Jesus my Lord. Amen.*

After praying this prayer it would be good to offer a Mass for the deceased members of your family. At this Mass, you could receive Communion in their name, asking Jesus to bring them total freedom and peace, and to heal any remaining generational bondage.

Even though we are attacked in the weakest areas of our lives, we must remember that we are not powerless. We have the power of the Blood of Jesus Christ to help us. And Jesus has given us authority over Satan. When we are sick, we take precautions so that we will not get worse. We also take medicine to help us to get better. When we are involved in a spiritual battle within ourselves, we first must know what part of our lives is besieged. Whether it is low self-esteem, temptation, a weakened conscience, or sin-based oppression, it is important to realize the locus of the battle. Then we can, united with Jesus, confront the enemy, knowing that we will be victorious. United with Jesus, we can withstand any onslaught that Satan hurls against us.

We not only have an attack against us within, but a battle rages all around us as well. Satan tries to confront us on all sides to wear us down. In the outward attack, he tries to discourage us and weaken us through our own sinful flesh and the world so that we will not have the energy to follow God's call.

SEVEN

The Battle around Us

A couple of months ago I went to St. Philip the Apostle Church in Pasadena to give a talk. I decided to leave Los Angeles at 6:30 that evening, hoping that all the traffic would be out of the city by that time. I got on the freeway and traffic was moving along when all of a sudden, I found myself caught in a big traffic jam. The freeway was like a huge parking lot, and I wasn't going anywhere fast.

After a short time, it became clear that I was going to be late, if I didn't miss it altogether. As I inched along the freeway, I decided to exit at the first available off-ramp and use side streets to get to the church. It took about seven minutes to travel the one mile to the off-ramp. I exited the freeway and pulled out my map. After plotting my new course, I finally arrived at the church, only fifteen minutes late.

There was no possible way to get to the parish on time taking the freeway. So I took another course. I used the side streets for my journey.

This is a good example of how Satan usually operates. He tries to attack us through low self-esteem, a weakened conscience, or through sin-based oppression. If he cannot attack us through these means, he will try another way. Just like my experience on the freeway, if Satan gets in a "spiritual traffic jam," he will use another method to try and take us away from God. If he does not succeed in attacking us internally (the battle within), he will attack us externally (the battle around us).

SATAN'S FLAMING ARROWS

Have you ever had sinful thoughts come into your mind for no apparent reason? It seems as if these thoughts suddenly appear out of nowhere. They are out of character, bizarre, and shocking. For example, having a sudden urge to steal, to be unfaithful to your spouse, or to engage in some violent or abusive behavior. These are not deliberate, planned thoughts, but impulsive and shocking. From where do these thoughts come? Sometimes we can wonder what is happening to us. Why am I plagued by these sinful thoughts? What is wrong with me?

Most of us are reasonable people. We do not have psychiatric disorders that would cause these thought patterns. Yet it seems that we are besieged by them at times. It is as if they never stop coming. It is as if something is attacking our minds *from without.* Paul says: "In addition to all this, take up the shield of faith, with which you can extinguish all the *flaming arrows* of the evil one" (Eph 6:16 italics mine).

We must remember that we live in not only a material world, but also in a spiritual world. There is an interaction between us and spiritual beings. We interact with Jesus Christ when we are in prayer and following his commands. We also interact with the demons of darkness when they try to draw us away from God.

Excessive or unfounded irritation, bitterness, lustful impulses, jealousy, fear, thoughts of suicide, doubt, rage, and hatred—all these thoughts are attacks upon us. The attack comes against our minds and emotions. Paul called these thoughts *flaming arrows.* Our own weaknesses can be triggered by certain tensions; Satan wishes to prey upon those areas.[1]

The flaming arrow by itself is not sinful. Its purpose is to lead us into sin; it becomes an agent of sin when we dwell on the thought. First we allow ourselves to think about it. Then as we dwell on it more and more, we begin to plan how to act upon it. Finally, we deliberately act upon what at first was only an inclination.

James describes this dynamic when he says: "But each one is tempted when, by his own evil desire, he is dragged away and enticed. Then, after desire has conceived, it gives birth to sin; and sin, when it is full-grown, gives birth to death" (Jas 1:14-15). But what is the difference between our own sinful tendency and a flaming arrow from Satan? How can we know if the battle is primarily from within or without?

This is difficult to discern. For me, I know my own sinful tendencies. My own sinful desire is familiar to me and has predictable patterns. That knowledge comes through prayer and allowing the Holy Spirit to convict me of my sins. The flaming arrow of Satan is different. This attack comes from outside of me. It is as if it comes from out of the blue, with a very strong intensity. It can be a one-time flaming arrow, or it can come repeatedly, with greater or lesser intensity.

How to deal with flaming arrows. The first step is to realize that this is not just my own sinful tendency. We need to pray to let the Holy Spirit convict us if this is from our own sinful nature. If it is a flaming arrow, we are to expose it for what it is—a lie, a trick of Satan. We bring this arrow to God's Word to expose it for the lie that it is. Once we know it is a lie, it is easier to deal with.

George came to me for counseling. He was obsessed with thoughts of infidelity in his marriage. He had severe temptations to go to prostitutes. He was happy in his marriage, but these thoughts would seem to flood him at odd times. He was never unfaithful, but it was getting more difficult to get rid of these thoughts.

I told him that sometimes it is not enough to just identify the lie. We must also take a stand against these thoughts. Paul says, "We demolish arguments and every pretension that sets itself up against the knowledge of God, and we take captive every thought to make it obedient to Christ" (2 Cor 10:5).

I told George to put this passage of Scripture into practice. Every time he had this kind of thought he was to pray, "Jesus, I take authority over this thought and I make it captive to you." I told him to do this for one month, then to come back and see me. The month passed and George came to see me. He told me that he was no longer besieged by these thoughts of infidelity. The more he made those thoughts captive to Christ, the less those thoughts plagued him. When we make the flaming arrows of Satan captive to Jesus Christ, these sorts of attacks will eventually leave.

SPIRITUAL CONTAMINATION

I was doing some research on aspects of the occult. A friend of mine told me to go to the Bodhi Tree. I went to this store and was both shocked and amazed at all of the occult books I found. As I walked through this store, I started to get tired. I thought it was because of the long drive in traffic to get there. Finally, I got all the things that I needed for my research.

I walked out of the store and got into my car. I felt tired— but it was a strange kind of tiredness. I felt that I was spiritually drained. I had prayed before entering the store and covered myself with the Blood of Christ. But there was so much evil in that store that I still felt spiritually contaminated.

I sat in my car for a few minutes and prayed. I put on some

Christian music to help lift my spirit. As I sang with the music, I began to feel a strengthening in my spirit. It was as if things were clinging to me from the store. As I prayed and sang praises to God, these things began to lift.

I shared this experience with a couple of friends. As we prayed, we realized that the evil spirits in the store tried to harass and attack me. That was why I felt spiritually drained. Through the praise of God, the evil spirits were forced to flee.

Sometimes we can have a similar feeling after being with a person or a group of people. There is a certain spiritual presence around those who have been involved in the occult, a presence not from the Holy Spirit. After spending time with them, we may feel tired or spiritually drained. Whenever I pray for deliverance, I always have someone pray over me asking that Jesus remove any "spiritual contamination" that may be affecting me.

Dealing with spiritual contamination. When we are feeling spiritually drained, we need to set aside time for prayer, asking the Holy Spirit to reveal the root of the contamination. Sometimes I will review my day with the Holy Spirit, asking his guidance to examine what happened in every appointment that I had.

One day a woman who was depressed asked me to pray for her. It was about one o'clock in the afternoon. We prayed, and she felt better and left. Later, about three o'clock, I felt that I had no energy. That is strange for me because I usually experience a surge of energy in the afternoons.

As the day wore on, I was becoming more tired. It was as if I was becoming depressed. I had a lot of work to do that evening. I would not be able to do it in my present state. I began to pray and review my day with the Holy Spirit. In a couple of minutes, the Holy Spirit revealed to me that I had been spiritually contaminated during the appointment that I had earlier with the

depressed woman. I then asked Jesus to remove this depression
and fill me with his peace and joy. Instantaneously, I felt a lifting
and my energy level increased.

As we review our day with the Holy Spirit, he will inform us
if we have been spiritually contaminated. If this has happened,
we come before Jesus, renouncing any contamination that happened in the name of Jesus and asking him to cleanse us with
his precious Blood. After this prayer, we can invite Jesus to
pour a fresh anointing of the Holy Spirit upon us.

In spiritual warfare we also battle against the world and the
flesh. We not only face the flaming arrows of Satan and spiritual
contamination; the world and the flesh are areas that Satan can
use to dissuade us from following God.

THE WORLD

In the theological sense of the word, according to St. Paul
and the author of the letters of John, the world is a society that
does not acknowledge the sovereignty of God. The world
stands in opposition to God. "Do not love the world.... If anyone loves the world, love for the Father is not in him" (1 Jn
2:15). "For the wisdom of this world is foolishness in God's
sight" (1 Cor 3:19). The basis of opposition to God is found in
the sinfulness of the world, and this sin entered the world
through the sin of Adam and Eve.

The world is hostile to God, but God is not hostile to the
world. In Christ, God reconciles the world to himself (2 Cor
5:19). As long as the world remains unredeemed, Christians
cannot identify with it. Jesus comes to redeem the world, but
he is not part of the world. The world is loved so much by God
that he sent his only Son to redeem it (Jn 3:16). Jesus is the
Lamb of God who takes away the sin of the world (Jn 1:29).

In the Gospel of John, the world is anti-God. It does not

recognize Jesus nor the Father (Jn 1:10; 17:25). Who is the ruler of this world? Some people interpret this term as Satan, others state that the ruler of the world is a collective personification of humanity unredeemed and hostile to God which sets itself up as an opposing power.[3]

The disciples, although they are called to live in the world, are not to be part of the world. Jesus himself does not pray for the world. He prays for *the disciples who are in the world.* Jesus himself overcomes the world and has broken the world's power (Jn 16:33). The disciples also overcome the world by their faith (1 Jn 5:4) which refuses to acknowledge the power of the world and thus reduces it to impotence.[4]

In the New Testament, the world is in opposition to God. God originally created the world as good. Because of the fall through the sin of Adam and Eve, original sin entered the world and it became hostile to God. Christians, like Jesus, are in the world and have a mission to the world and overcome it by the love of God. They are not to identify with the world, but they cannot lose their identity with the world either as the creation of God.

THE FLESH

The most common usage of the word flesh in the New Testament is to identify men and women as sinners. The flesh does not necessarily mean the human body. It is the sin inherent in our fallen humanity, our lust and desires that lead us away from God. "For the sinful nature desires what is contrary to the Spirit, and the Spirit what is contrary to the sinful nature. They are in conflict with each other" (Gal 5:17).

The flesh is morally weak and one who serves the flesh serves the law of sin (Rom 7:25). To set the mind on the flesh is death, it is enmity to God and the flesh cannot please God

(Rom 8:6). Those who belong to Jesus must crucify the flesh with its passions and desires (Gal 5:24). The flesh and the spirit are in opposition to each other. He who sows in the flesh reaps corruption, but he who sows for the spirit reaps eternal life (Gal 5:16).

As we have seen, the flesh does not mean the physical body. Nor is it to be equated with sexual desires alone. The flesh is any tendency in human beings which would lead us away from God. These sinful tendencies, as we saw in the earlier chapter, are a part of us. They are a result of the fall. We struggle against them and Satan aggravates them, but through the power of the cross we are victorious over them.

THE WORLD, THE FLESH, AND THE DEVIL

Chapter three discussed Satan and his nature, and we have discussed in this chapter the flaming arrows he sends our way. He wishes to attack us. His goal is to drive us away from God. He uses the world and the flesh to his advantage. Remember that the world is in opposition to God and the flesh is also in opposition to God. These are not the realms of the Spirit. Also Christians are to live in the world, but not identify with the world. Christians cannot separate themselves from their existence in the flesh, but they are expected to have mastery over the flesh.

The point is, Satan wishes to aggravate certain weaknesses in our lives. He tries to tempt us in these areas when we are worn down by our own flesh and the allurements of the world. Our antidote is living a life centered on God. To be centered on God means that we must be people of prayer. When we let go of our prayer life, we become susceptible to the attack that Satan leashes against us from the world and our own flesh.

For example, some days we may not have sufficient time to

pray. We can get involved in many things. It could be pressing work that must be done in our everyday world, or maybe an emergency occurs. We become involved in the emergency at hand or over involved in our work. Slowly other things start to take up too much of our time and we begin to pray less and less. Soon, our own flesh and the cares of the world have crowded out God and the flaming arrows of Satan seem to increase in number. Then we wonder why God doesn't seem to be there when we call and why it is so hard to fight off temptations.

Or let's take another scenario. We have to work in order to have enough money to live. The economy is not good, taxes are being raised, and we may lose our job if we do not put in extra hours. The more we work, the less time we have with our families. And it's likely that if we have less time for our families, we also will have less time for our relationship with God. We may begin to get depressed because of our lack of time with loved ones. This lack of time depresses us. Then we may begin to doubt God's protection over us. We doubt his love and care. So we pray less and less and may even stop attending Sunday Mass.

In both of these scenarios Satan is setting the stage for an assault. He allows the troubles of everyday life to begin to take a toll on us. When this happens we begin to get tired and depressed. When all our time is being taken up with making sure that we have food on the table and a place to live, our spiritual life begins to suffer. All of our energy is sucked away by worldly concerns.

We begin to become more and more part of the world, the world that does not acknowledge the sovereignty of God. We become emotionally empty and depressed. We feel no consolation even when we do pray. We cry out to God, but we think that he does not hear our prayer because things don't change. We begin to assume that God does not answer our prayers and perhaps doesn't even care.

Since we believe that God does not answer our prayers, we lose hope in his promises as well. We then place our hope and more of our energy in the world and pursuing our own fleshly pursuits. We rarely pray. We discover to our frustration, though, that our selfish lifestyle brings no satisfaction. We have no peace. Satan then makes his move against us because we are in a severely weakened position.

He may tempt us with alcohol and drugs to deaden the pain. He may entice us to seek a sexual relationship outside our marriage because of the difficulties in our homes. As we begin to entertain these temptations, we pray even less and seek ways to deaden the pain, depression, and sadness. Satan then draws us deeper into his web of evil and perhaps we fall into a pattern of serious sin.

In such a weakened state, some people will leave the Christian life and walk only in the ways of the world. Some will become addicted to alcohol. Some will be lured into the occult or New Age Movement. Some will commit serious sexual sin. And some will become so depressed that they will try to commit suicide.

But this does not have to happen. We have power over the Evil One! Even when we are in the throes of alcoholism, despair, and on the brink of suicide, we have a way out. That way out is repentance and professing our faith in Jesus Christ! We must reclaim what Satan is trying to steal. Jesus is always willing to save the sinner. No sin is too great. Jesus is waiting for us to come to him, to let him bear our sorrows.

These scenarios have happened to people I know, and suspect you know, too. To make sure that they do not happen to us, we must live a life of prayer. Our relationship with God must become and remain the most important thing in our lives. We must put God first. On a talk about prayer to priests, Fr. Michael Scanlan said: "If you do not have enough time to pray during the day, get up earlier." If we are saying that we are too busy to pray, then we must get up earlier and use that time to pray. Daily prayer is the greatest weapon we have to thwart the attack of Satan.

DAILY STRUGGLES

Even with a commitment to daily prayer, we will experience problems because we are involved in the spiritual battle. Satan does not need to attack those who are not following God. He already has them in his grasp. Therefore, he focuses his attacks on those who are trying to follow God, using not only his own flaming arrows but the weakness of the flesh and the wiles of the world as well.

Whenever we experience a trial, we have a choice: we can break down, giving in to doubts about God's promise or purpose in pain; or we can hold steady, breaking through to a deeper level of character. Paul himself was besieged with trials: "To keep me from being conceited because of these surpassingly great revelations, there was given me a thorn in my flesh, a messenger of Satan, to torment me. Three times I pleaded with the Lord to take it away from me. But he said to me, 'My grace is sufficient for you, for my power is made perfect in weakness'" (2 Cor 12:7-9).

The purpose of Paul's suffering was to help him grow in his spiritual life and to assist him in his ministry. Paul did not look for suffering, but since God had promised to use it for his glory, Paul endured it. "Suffering produces perseverance; perseverance, character; and character, hope" (Rom 5:3-4). Christians will suffer. We do not like it, but God can and does use it for our spiritual growth.

St. John of the Cross and St. Teresa of Avila both speak about the "dark night of the soul." This can be a time when we feel totally abandoned by God. But we must endure through this struggle to reach a deeper union with God. The most important part of a particular suffering or hardship is to see if you can discern God's purpose in it.

In your struggle against sin, you have not yet resisted to the point of shedding your blood. And you have forgotten that word of encouragement that addresses you as sons: "My son, do not make light of the Lord's discipline, and do not lose heart when he rebukes you, because the Lord disciplines those he loves, and he punishes everyone he accepts as a son."

Endure hardship as discipline; God is treating you as sons. For what son is not disciplined by his father? If you are not disciplined (and everyone undergoes discipline), then you are illegitimate children and not true sons. Moreover, we have all had human fathers who disciplined us and we respected them for it. How much more should we submit to the Father of our spirits and live!

Our fathers disciplined us for a little while as they thought best; but God disciplines us for our good, that we may share in his holiness. No discipline seems pleasant at the time, but painful. Later on, however, it produces a harvest of righteousness and peace for those who have been trained by it.

Hebrews 12:4-11

If God intends to use the suffering for his purposes, then we will receive the grace to endure it with a peaceful heart. If we recognize that it is not part of his plan for us, then we should resolve to get rid of it.

How can we understand God's will in our suffering? Some suffering is due to our own human nature; some suffering can be an attack from the Evil One. It takes the wisdom and guidance of the Holy Spirit to discern the source of suffering in our lives. When the source of the problem is our own human weakness, it may be God's way of disciplining us and molding our character. But if Satan is preying upon those weaknesses and trying to destroy our peace of mind, we know it is demonic oppression. We should always take authority in Jesus' name over such oppression in our lives. Mary's story in the next chapter is an example of how demonic oppression can influence our lives.

8

How Demonic Oppression Works

The symptoms do not seem that bad. At first there is tired-ness and a shortness of breath. Then various parts of the body may begin to ache. The blood does not clot as well as it used to, and there is a tendency to bruise easily. It could be that you have a vitamin deficiency, or it could be something else. These minor problems may be symptoms of acute leukemia, a potentially deadly cancer.

Though the outward signs do not seem that bad, inside the body is under siege. Cancerous cells have invaded the bone marrow and bloodstream. The body no longer produces enough healthy white blood cells, taking away the body's abil-ity to fight off infections.

Suddenly the person feels very sick and needs immediate medical attention. Untreated, a person can die in six weeks. Treatment can involve intravenous chemotherapy with drugs that kill not only cancerous cells, but normal cells as well. The hope is that only healthy cells will grow again after treatment.

Like leukemia, evil can spread quickly and remain largely unnoticed. Yet it is deadly and difficult to get rid of. Look at our own experience of how the siege or onslaught begins. It starts with a temptation to disobey the laws of God. We might think it is not that bad; everyone else does it. Who will know about it? I'll do it just once. We fail to realize that evil has now been perpetrated and has taken root within us.

The sinful action, if it goes unchecked, acts like a spiritual cancer, spreading into other areas of our lives. We find it easier to sin. Our prayer becomes less frequent. Physical problems may even develop because we do not want to face honestly our open rebellion to God.

Though we know we are in the wrong, we rationalize our rebellion. We continue to stay in a sinful way of living or repeatedly fall into the same pattern of sin. We begin to believe that God will never forgive us. Mistakenly we believe that our suffering is a punishment from God. In reality, we are suffering because we choose to run away from God's protection.

Finally, we stop praying and reading the Bible altogether, because when we pray we are reminded of our sin. We may try to ask for God's forgiveness. But if we continue living in sin, in open rebellion to the laws of God, our prayers will not be answered since we have left God's protection.

Some people may come in to our lives to try to help us. We may refuse their help because they challenge us to live the truth of God's Word. Eventually we turn away from them since their words convict us. We refuse to change our ways, and it becomes clear that the evil has permeated our spiritual lives.

Yet we must always remember that God is loving and forgiving if we will but turn to him with sincerity of heart. Just when it seems that we will totally reject God and his commands, something wonderful happens. God chooses to send a special grace into our lives as a result of another person's faithful prayers. This one person, whom we may never know, has been interceding on our behalf. In response to their prayers, God sends us his Spirit to call us back to himself. If the Holy Spirit is received by us and we repent, God renews and heals us. If we reject the movement of his Spirit, we may end up losing our salvation.

Like cancer, evil can be stopped with the proper medication. God's medications are prayer, fasting, and repentance. As we use God's medications, we will leave behind the evil things that we did and be strengthened anew to follow the will of God.

MARY'S STORY

Mary and Joe had been married for twelve years. They had experienced some problems in their marriage, but they were dedicated to each other and wanted to work through them together. Mary had graduated from cosmetology school over two years ago and was helping supplement the family income.

Mary's brother-in-law knew that they could use a little extra money, so he told them about Bill, who needed a place to stay. Mary and Joe talked about the possibility of Bill living in one of their spare bedrooms and paying rent. So they decided to offer Bill a room, which he accepted. For the first three months everything seemed to go well. They provided housing for Bill and the rent he paid them was helping financially.

One day Bill asked Mary if he could read her palm. Mary told him that she did not believe in palm reading, but Bill persisted. Finally, Mary gave in and Bill read her palm. Then Bill told her that her husband, Joe, was having an affair. Bill described the physical appearance of this other woman—the color of her hair, her eyes, and her height. He said this woman was working where Joe was employed, but Mary refused to believe it.

Bill then told Mary that he would read tarot cards to show her that he was telling the truth. He read the tarot cards four times, each time coming up with the same information about the alleged affair. After this, Mary found it very difficult to sleep. She became depressed and would suddenly burst into tears. She even decided to follow her husband to his work to see if she could see the woman Bill described.

Mary never told Joe about the things that Bill did and said because she was afraid of his reaction. She felt ashamed for what she had done and ashamed that she was following him. She also did not want to accuse Joe of anything because she had no proof—only Bill's palm reading and tarot card reading. While Mary did not see anyone at Joe's work matching the description Bill gave, she still feared that he might be having an affair.

Bill then offered to help Mary. He told her he could do something to make sure that Joe would end the affair. He claimed that he helped other women with similar problems.

Bill told Mary that he needed certain things to help her. He told her to get some of Joe's hair and her hair and then wrap them together in her underwear. Then Bill "did something" to the underwear and told her to place the underwear under their bed. Mary did these things, but she did not find peace. She suffered intensely with the thoughts of the alleged infidelity of her spouse. She thought, "Maybe I'll get up early, put gas in the car, drive away, and never return." But this idea drove her into a deeper sense of fear and depression.

One day while Mary was working, someone told her about a person who might be able to help her. This man was a *santero*, a priest of Santeria which is a religion that has its origins with the Yoruba tribe of Africa. Between 1820 and 1840, the majority of slaves shipped from the ports of the Bight of Benin were Yoruba. These slaves were brought to Cuba and Brazil to work in the sugar plantations.

The Catholic practices of the Spaniards deeply influenced the Cuban Yoruba. The popular piety of Catholicism in Cuba was centered almost exclusively on the veneration of the saints. In their efforts to hide their magical and religious practices from the Spaniards, the Yoruba identified their African deities with the saints of the Catholic church. This was the beginning of *Santeria*.

The Yoruba gradually adapted to complement and reflect the Catholic worldview. Through this accommodation *Santeria* emerged, the way of the saints, because the devotions to the *orishas* (African gods) were carried out beneath the images of the Catholic saints.

Santeria came to the United States in 1959, at the time of the Cuban revolution. Since that time over one million Cubans have left the island as political exiles. Among these people were santerian priests and priestessses. The priests of the religion use divination to discern the destiny of an individual and to discern if someone is experiencing problems that are rooted in an evil. After these things have been discerned, sorcery (magic) is used to encourage a good destiny or to cleanse from evil.

A Catholic must be particularly careful because *Santeria* tries to blend some aspects of the Catholic faith into its beliefs. In the *botanicas* (santerian stores), one will find traditional Catholic articles next to the articles of *Santeria*. Be forewarned: the Catholic faith *is not* compatible with the worldview of *Santeria*.

The *santero* told Mary that Bill was wrong, that there was no other woman in her husband's life. He said that he would do something to help her have peace of mind, but Mary still did not have peace. Whenever Mary and Joe went out to dinner or dancing, she would look at other women, wondering if her husband was attracted to them. The idea of Joe's infidelity became so fearful to her that she did not trust any other woman.

Every time that he was late coming home from work, she would get very jealous. They began fighting more, and their relationship began to deteriorate. Mary started praying, begging God for peace and asking him to remove the jealousy and thoughts of her husband's infidelity. She began to attend prayer groups, hoping to find peace. She and her husband even went on retreats together. Still she had these nagging thoughts and suspicions.

One day Joe went to the garage to get some light bulbs. He was in the garage for about ten minutes. Suddenly Mary was overcome with fear that he was with another woman in their garage. Mary went to the garage, and the car was not there. But Joe returned in about ten minutes. He explained that he had gone to the store because there were no light bulbs in the garage.

That night Mary lay awake thinking about the incident. The next day she went to see a friend who was a spiritualist. A spiritualist is a person who contacts spiritual beings or the spirits of people who have died. They try to find information from these spirits to assist their clients. Spiritualists believe that the spirits live in another dimension or plane of existence. They believe that these spirits can help us, but they also admit that some of these spirits wish to harm us. She told the spiritualist all that was happening in her life and in her relationship with her husband. The spiritualist told her that there was a woman who was very interested in her husband. Mary, when she returned home, confronted Joe with this new information.

He denied the allegation and was very angry that Mary thought that he was being unfaithful to her. She did not believe him. The spiritualist also told Mary that she could help her solve her problem with her husband. First, she was to tell Bill to move out of their house, which he did. Then she was to bring some personal item of her husband to her, so she could do some ritual to resolve the problem.

The ritual was performed, but things seemed to get only worse. Mary wanted a divorce, but she was afraid to live alone. The following week a member of her prayer group mentioned my name to her. Mary called and asked for an appointment. She and her husband came to see me on Friday afternoon. I spoke with both Mary and Joe to assess what was happening in their relationship. Mary told me about Bill, the *santero*, and the spiritualist. I explained to her and Joe that these people and their actions were not from God. They were involved in the occult. I proceeded to explain Satan's deceptions and how Satan had tried to destroy their marriage.

But the explanation of how Satan tried to destroy their marriage was not enough. We needed to break the bondage of the occult in Mary's life. She was involved in the occult through palm reading, tarot cards, the *santero*, and the spiritualist. Through them she had participated in divination and witchcraft. We needed God's remedy of repentance and prayer to bring her freedom from the evil in which she had participated.

I asked her husband to leave my office because she needed to go to confession. After her confession, I invited her husband back into my office. I then led her in a prayer of renunciation of her involvement in the occult. I asked her to repeat after me, "In the name of Jesus, I renounce my involvement in palm reading, tarot cards, *Santeria*, spiritualism, and any other form of divination, witchcraft, or sorcery that I have done." After that prayer, I had her reaffirm her baptismal vows. I then prayed a prayer of deliverance and inner healing for her.

When I began to pray, her head began to rotate from side to side. Then she got a headache and her vision blurred. After I commanded Satan to leave her alone, the manifestation stopped. I asked Jesus to fill her with the Holy Spirit. With that prayer she became very peaceful. I asked the Lord to continue to work in her life and to heal her psychological wounds.

After this time of prayer, I asked Mary and Joe to forgive each other for the accusations and fighting over the past months. Then I prayed that God would heal their marriage. One month after this experience, I called Mary to see how they were doing. Mary told me that the thoughts of infidelity had stopped, and she and her husband were able to live in peace with each other.

God's medicine worked. Through repentance and prayer, Mary was rescued from demonic oppression. Her marriage was healed. She now lives in peace and is very careful not to allow Satan a foothold in her life through participation in the occult.

ROOT CAUSES OF PROBLEMS

In Mary's story there were two root causes for her marital problems. The first was the financial stress that Joe and Mary were experiencing. This stress caused tension in their relationship. It was the reason why they invited Bill to rent a room from them. The second root was Bill himself. He introduced Mary to the occult through the palm reading, tarot cards, and witchcraft.

As Mary progressed deeper and deeper into the occult, she experienced greater problems in her marriage and was unable to live in peace. Mary's story demonstrates that many of our problems are a combination of various things. Our difficulties can be human or spiritual, or a combination of both. In Mary's case Satan attacked a challenging human situation and caused great psychological and emotional disturbances in her life through her occult involvement. Satan is always eager to aggravate an existing problem or weakness in our lives.

Spiritual causes. Sometimes our problems can be a result of a troubled spiritual life. For example, if we are living in unforgiveness, bitterness, and hatred, we will not be able to receive the fullness of God's blessings and will open ourselves to demonic oppression. Our unforgiveness can be directed toward God or other people.

If we are angry at God, we need to "forgive" him. To "forgive" God means that I am willing to accept his movement in my life. Sometimes we believe that God does not hear our prayers. We become angry at God for not taking care of us. We are in suffering and as we call out to God we believe that he refuses to hear our prayers. We forget that the suffering we endure is a means of growth.

When we "forgive" God, we are letting go of our anger at him. I use the word "forgive" with quotes because when we say I forgive, I refer to something psychological that happens within us. It is a more powerful word than saying I let go or I accept. In "forgiving" God and accepting his movement in our lives, we become reconciled to him. Often we do not understand why he allows suffering. We fail to see his purpose and will, especially when we are in the midst of it. In our lack of understanding, we may harbor a grudge against God for allowing us to experience a particular suffering. We may feel that God has treated us unjustly.

For example, if a member of our family dies suddenly, we may be angry at the perpetrator of the act and God. When my fifteen-year-old niece died of cancer, I was very angry at God. I asked him why he did not hear our prayers to heal her. I never got an answer. The only course of action for me is to accept his will, trusting that he knows what is best for me and my family.

When tragedy strikes we often ask, "Why me? What have I done to deserve this?" We may never know why in this life. We do not understand why God allows people to get hurt. But God can and does use suffering for our personal growth. Maybe examining the wisdom of parents with their children will help us to understand why.

Parents allow their children to make mistakes, so they can learn to distinguish right from wrong. Sometimes the decisions that their children make will hurt them, but prudent parents do not always intervene and stop children from hurting themselves. Sometimes a child must learn "the hard way." Parents give their children rules for living. If they do not follow those rules, they may get hurt. It is the same with God. God allows us to get hurt sometimes, so we can grow to be responsible Christians.

We may make wrong decisions and get hurt, either as individuals or as a community. God has given us free will and will not force us to make good moral decisions. He will not force us to follow his laws. But he will allow us to undergo suffering in order to grow in wisdom, so we hopefully will not repeat the same error or sin.

After we "forgive" God, it is important to forgive our earthly father and mother. All of us have unconscious anger toward our parents because they were not perfect. But we must remember that they do love us and they probably did the best they could in raising us. Some people have even suffered abuse from their parents or siblings. We need to realize that the call to forgive does not excuse the abuse. They are still responsible for their actions.

But through forgiveness, we are able to understand that their actions may have been driven by their own pain and suffering. They were probably driven by emotions of anger, bitterness, and desire for revenge—perhaps rooted in their own upbringing. We do have a choice: to forgive or to harbor bitterness in our hearts. If we choose to sow seeds of anger, revenge, bitterness, and hate, we will reap the undesirable fruit of emotional instability, negativism that ruins relationships, and physical illness such as cancer, arthritis, diabetes, and the like.[1] Satan may well develop a stronghold in our lives, and we may begin to experience demonic oppression as well.

God's solution to our bitterness and resentments is forgiveness. As we forgive, God heals our hurts and we can live in peace. Again, forgiveness does not mean that the hurt did not happen. It does not necessarily mean that I have to like the perpetrator of the abuse. Forgiveness means that I decide to forgive this person's actions toward me. Forgiveness is an act of the will. It is not a feeling. Through forgiveness I can be freed to live a fuller life in God. Remember the Our Father: "Forgive us our trespasses as we forgive those who trespass against us."

We need to recall the Scripture, Ephesians 4:26-27, which states, "'In your anger do not sin.' Do not let the sun go down while you are still angry, and do not give the devil a foothold." We are encouraged to "get rid of all bitterness, rage and anger, brawling and slander, along with every form of malice. Be kind and compassionate to one another, forgiving each other, just as in Christ God forgave you" (Eph 4:31-32).

Finally, we must also forgive ourselves. If we are going to forgive others, we must also forgive ourselves. We commonly say, "I am going to forgive myself so that I can forgive you." If we are going to take a loving concern for others, we must also take a loving concern for ourselves.

Another source of spiritual problems is unconfessed sin. If we are living in a sinful situation and refusing to change our lives, we will reap our own spiritual destruction. For example, if we are living in adultery and we refuse to leave the person, we place ourselves in grave spiritual danger, "for God will judge the adulterer and all the sexually immoral" (Heb 13:4). Deliberately living in opposition to the laws of God will bring spiritual oppression to our lives.

Since we are fighting a spiritual battle, we need to be spiritually nourished. We must read the Word of God in Scripture, pray each day, and keep the Lord's Day holy through sharing in Sunday Mass. If we do not grow spiritually in these ways, we will not be strong enough to follow God's will in times of trial.

Our faith may be shaken. We might doubt that God is in control of everything and that he can bring good out of evil. We need the strength of the Holy Spirit that comes from prayer to resist the temptations of the Evil One. We need the Sacrament of Reconciliation (confession) to receive forgiveness for our sins and the grace to change our lives.

Psychological and emotional causes. Our life history can affect our relationships. If we have suffered rejection and abandonment in our childhood, it will be difficult for us to have open and honest relationships. Divorce can affect our ability to trust. Alcoholic parents or physical, emotional, or sexual abuse may cripple us emotionally. We may be living in fear, guilt, shame, or inferiority. We may have been victimized as children.

A victim is anyone who has been physically, sexually, emotionally, or spiritually exploited through either overt or covert aggression or control. Physical or emotional abandonment constitutes victimization as well. Many professionals suggest that the trauma of abuse leads to psychological, emotional, and social difficulties of all kinds.[2]

There are three basic questions to life: (1) Who am I? (2) What is my purpose? and (3) What must I do to be safe? If we grew up in a healthy environment, receiving all the love we needed, we will have a healthy self-image. We will be able to love unselfishly and be able to receive love in a healthy manner. If our parents were Christians, we will grow up understanding that we are made in God's image and we have the right to become the people God created us to be.

The following are some characteristics of a healthy family:

1. It is balanced; it can adapt to change.
2. Problems are handled on a family basis, not just an individual basis.
3. There are solid cross-generational connections.
4. Clear boundaries are maintained between individuals.
5. People deal with each other directly.
6. Differences are accepted and encouraged.
7. The thoughts and feelings of others are accepted.
8. Individuals know what they can give to, and receive from, others.
9. Maintaining a positive emotional climate is a high priority.

10. Each family member values the family as "a good place to live."
11. Each learns from the others and encourages feedback.
12. Individuals are allowed to experience their own emptiness.[3]

But if we grew up in an unhealthy atmosphere, we will experience deep problems in relationships. We will not be able to trust another person's love for us. We may wish to punish ourselves because we believe that we are not worthy of anyone's love, including God's.

In his book *Healing the Shame that Binds You*, John Bradshaw states that when we grow up in a dysfunctional family system, we can be victims of toxic shame. As we have seen, this is different from guilt. Healthy guilt is the emotional core of our conscience. It is the emotion which results from behaving in a manner contrary to our beliefs and values. Healthy guilt is part of our normal psychological makeup. It helps us set the right kinds of boundaries, with the realization that we are finite human beings with clear limitations. Healthy shame says that we will make mistakes. It is a normal part of life and we are not bad because we make mistakes.

Toxic shame is different. If we are living with toxic shame, we believe that we *are* a mistake, we *are* no good, and we *are* worthless. We believe that we are defective and flawed, that there is nothing that we can do to change. The situation is hopeless.[4] We get toxic shame through abandonment, rejection, and abuse (the abuse can be verbal, physical, emotional, or sexual) from our primary family system.

The following is a list of dysfunctional family rules:

1. *We do not feel.* We keep our emotions guarded, especially anger (though often there is one person who is allowed to express feelings openly, especially anger).

2. *We are always in control.* We do not show weakness. We do not ask for help, which is a sign of weakness.

3. *We deny what is going on.* We do not believe our senses or perceptions. We lie to ourselves and to others.

4. *We do not trust.* Not ourselves, not others. No one can be relied upon, no one can be confided in.

5. *We keep the family's secrets.* Even if we told, no one would believe us—or so we think.

6. *We are ashamed.* We are to blame for everything bad that happens—and we deserve it.[5]

Psychological disorders can be responsible for some problems. Phobias and anxieties attack our peace. Anxiety attacks usually come from our life experiences of abuse or neglect, a chemical deficiency, or a personality disorder. Obsessive-compulsive thoughts and behaviors, or compulsive addictions like alcoholism, gambling, and eating disorders, are behavioral patterns. Sometimes Satan can influence and exacerbate such an addiction. Once the bondage is broken, the life issues that primarily caused the addiction need to be examined and remedied.

Clinical depression can be caused by a chemical imbalance. Sometimes proper medication brings great relief and enables progress in therapy. Schizophrenia can be caused by a combination of genetic and environmental factors. In all of these situations, a demonic presence can be present which exacerbates underlying emotional problems. Breaking of the bondage helps in the therapeutic process.

Physiological causes. Organic brain syndromes will affect a person's ability to function. Biochemical imbalances of the body chemistry can cause some problems. For example, premenstrual syndrome, menopause, postpartum depression, manic-depression, Epstein-Barr virus, and hypoglycemia can affect our moods. Stress and fatigue also affect our ability to think clearly. An unhealthy diet and lack of exercise can make us lethargic and confused. It is important to have a proper diet, rest, and exercise to be physically, mentally, and spiritually healthy.

Circumstantial causes. Things that happen in our everyday lives have an effect upon us. If there is a marital problem, it will affect the whole family. Financial problems put strains on relationships, as with Joe and Mary. That is especially prevalent today when people are losing their jobs due to the retooling of the economy. Personal tragedies, such as death or serious illness, affect our lives. Sometimes even the weather can affect how we feel. Daily news of wars, robberies, murders, drugs, and the like affect our lifestyles. It is extremely difficult to raise children in the Lord with such a constant barrage of materialistic and hedonistic values.

There are times when all of the above factors contribute to the problems that we have in our lives. As I stated before, Satan is always eager to aggravate our sufferings. In order to know the root causes of our problems, we must examine all the possible causes of our difficulties. To do this we need the gift of discernment.

THE IMPORTANCE OF DISCERNMENT

Whenever we are experiencing a problem, we must remember that the problems can be multi-layered. There may be a combination of physical, mental, emotional, and spiritual components to the problem. It would be wrong to try and solve a problem psychologically if the problem was primarily physical. If you are sick with the flu, you take aspirin and other medications for the flu and rest. You do not need therapy to solve a problem of the flu.

If the problem is mainly psychological, then a spiritual solution will be ineffective. We must be aware of this. Many times I have people come to me saying that they have a problem with a demonic oppression. When someone claims they are oppressed by a demon, they usually are not. They are giving too much power to Satan and refusing to examine their own issues which can be explained and helped by counseling.

And even when the problem is spiritual, we many times give in to the temptation. We are challenged to take some responsibility for our situation. For example, a person came to me claiming that he was oppressed by a spirit of lust. He said he couldn't control himself. Part of his problem was that he was refusing to fight this oppression on a spiritual or psychological level. We do have a choice in whether we follow temptation or not. For this person who had the spirit of lust, I asked him, "Who gets the most pleasure out of the lust, you or the demonic spirit?"

We must be careful in this area. We do not want to treat a psychological problem with a spiritual solution, nor do we want to treat a spiritual problem with a psychological solution. Where there is a multidimensional problem we need both the psychological solution (which is counseling) and the spiritual solution (inner healing and prayer).

Also, whenever we are talking about using discernment it is wise to seek group discernment because sometimes one person may be off base with a particular word of knowledge in prayer for inner healing. That is why we are cautioned to "test the spirits to see whether they are from God" (1 Jn 4:1). A person who has the word of knowledge or the gift of discernment of spirits is not right 100 percent of the time. Even the saints made mistakes in spiritual discernment. With this in mind, let us examine discernment.

To discern is to know or sift apart the characteristics of a certain situation. Discernment is the ability to understand the positives and negatives of a certain situation and come to a correct conclusion. Spiritual discernment is the ability to be led by the Holy Spirit in making a decision or resolving a problem. God knows perfectly, clearly, and totally. He gives us the gift of discernment to help us to understand things with his wisdom. Spiritual warfare is ineffective and potentially hazardous without spiritual discernment—the ability to see where, how, and when God desires to engage the enemy.[6]

In spiritual discernment there are three levels: human intuition, a supernatural endowment available to all believers, and a gift of discernment of spirits.[7] Some people have an uncanny ability to know the character traits of an individual. They simply are able to sense what a person is like. Is there a time when you just did not feel right about what someone was saying? That can be normal human intuition at work.

Sometimes we may have an ability to know something about a certain subject. We "innately" know. There is no real explanation for this ability. It is simply human intuition. I have a friend who can sense a particular quality about a person when she is talking to him or her. I believe that all of us have this human intuition to some degree. Some of us are more in touch with this ability than others.

The second level of discernment is a general supernatural endowment. When we become Christians, we receive the Holy Spirit. The Holy Spirit dwells in us and gives us many gifts. Paul prays for the Philippians: "And this is my prayer: that your love may abound more and more in knowledge and depth of insight, so that you may be able to discern what is best and may be pure and blameless until the day of Christ" (Phil 1:9-10).

As we grow in knowledge of God and his Word, we will be more aware of the call of God for our lives. General discernment is an endowment of the Holy Spirit to every believer, enabling him or her to perceive personally the grace of God which is available to help the person become holy and avoid evil.[8] This gift helps us to know the ways of God.

Even though we have this gift of discernment, Satan can rob us of it. This happens when we refuse to follow the guidance of the Holy Spirit. Satan may attack our thoughts, giving us reasons why we should not follow God's plan. This is rationalization; we make excuses for not being able to follow God's command-ments. Sometimes because of our own pain and hurt, we may disobey the laws of God.

But if we are open to the Holy Spirit and this gift of discern-ment, we will be brought to repentance. A very close friend of mine made a decision to live in a sinful situation. But when con-fronted with God's Word about his choices, he was convicted of his actions. He did not change immediately, but the Word of God kept gnawing at him. Finally he became open to the dis-cernment of the Holy Spirit. He repented and returned to God.

The third level of discernment is the charismatic gift of dis-cernment of spirits (1 Cor 12:10). This is the ability to distin-guish between spirits: the human spirit, the Spirit of God, and the evil spirit. In this gift God reveals to us the root cause of a situation. This gift grows within us as we grow in prayer.

It has been written: *There are paths which seem to man to be right, but which in the end lead him to hell.* To avoid this peril, St. John gives us these words of advice: *Test the spirits to see if they are from God.* Now no one can test the spirits to see if they are from God unless God has given him discernment of spirits to enable him to investigate spiritual thoughts, inclinations and intentions with honest and true judgment. Discernment is the mother of all virtues; everyone needs it either to guide the lives of others or to direct and reform his own life.

...We could see through any action of ours, or into our entire lives, if we had a simple eye.... This means that we see by right thinking what is to be done, and by our good intention we carry it out with simple honesty, because deceitful action is wrong. Right thinking does not permit mistakes; good intention rules out pretense. This then is true discernment, a combination of right thinking and good intention.[9]

As we grow in our relationship with God, we will grow in the gift of discernment on all three levels. I know that when I have a vibrant prayer life, I am more open to the movement of God in my life and able to make more use of his gift of discernment. I have learned to bring everything in my life to God for his wisdom and discernment.

A proper use of the gift of discernment is imperative when we are praying for inner healing. We must know the root causes of problems in order to minister to a person in the way in which God calls. Remember, to use the gift of discernment properly, we must humbly depend upon God.

To be in ministry without using the gift of discernment is harmful. For example, we may believe that a person is being harassed by a demonic spirit when the problem is physical or psychological in origin. We must wait for God to tell us when and how to move in a particular situation when ministering.

Remember that since Satan wishes to aggravate existing situations, he will try to harass the believer every chance he gets. The gift of discernment of spirits helps us to know when that harassment is taking place and when the situation is only spiritual, psychological, physiological, or circumstantial. The following story of Sally's healing demonstrates how sufferings in our lives can be multi-dimensional and how helpful discernment can be in sifting through them.

SALLY'S STORY

I met Sally about seven years ago. Sally was a twenty-five-year-old Catholic with a strong devotion to Mary. She prayed three rosaries a day, had been to Medjugorje, and even lived there for a year. Yet in spite of all her prayer and the support of friends, she felt that something was wrong. She did not feel good about herself. I could tell by the clothes that she wore that she did not care about her physical appearance.

Sally always wanted to be involved in the theater. She took dancing and acting classes, but the lifestyle that she found in the theater did not agree with her faith. There was so much pressure to commit sexual sin that she had to sacrifice her dream to be an actress. She was even pressured into some sexual relationships that were abusive. She felt that she deserved the abuse for not following the laws of God.

Sally had many personal problems. She believed that she was no good, that she was a mistake. It turned out that she was a victim of a dysfunctional family. Her father was abusive and an alcoholic. Her mother was not able to protect her from his angry outbursts because she too was afraid of him. Her mother was also emotionally distant from her throughout her childhood.

In addition, Sally was a victim of incest. She was made to feel dirty and ashamed. Incest can destroy the very core of a person. This was the case with Sally. She really believed that there was no possible way anyone could truly love her, even Jesus himself. Because of the abuse she had suffered through incest, her father's abusive personality, and the constant harassment of her brothers, she found it extremely difficult to relate to Jesus.

That is why Mary was so important for her. Through Mary she could have some relationship to God on a spiritual level. She could not trust Jesus, but she could trust Mary. I firmly believe that her devotion to Mary through the rosary protected her from tremendous harm. We must remember that Mary desires to bring us to Jesus. I believe that we are called to ask Jesus what type of relationship he wants us to have with his mother. We are then to develop the relationship with Mary that will help lead us to Jesus.

Sally did not have a proper diet. Sometimes she would not eat. When she did eat, she would only munch on junk food. She did not take proper care of her body and had no exercise regimen. Sally was not anorexic, but she was a possible candidate for this disease. Sometimes she did purposely throw up after an eating binge.

Sally had a deep-seated spiritual problem rooted in a sinful pattern of sexual relationships and her inability to relate to Jesus. She had emotional and psychological problems due to the abuse and incest she had suffered. She had physiological problems due to her lack of a healthy diet and failure to exercise. Her problems were multidimensional. But there was another problem that Sally had, something which would eventually lead her down a path of utter destruction and death.

Because of the abuse that she had experienced, Sally had made a pact with Satan. When she was twelve years old, she asked Satan for help because she believed that God had abandoned her. She was educated in a Catholic school, so she knew who Jesus was. But she believed that Jesus was not protecting her from her father's abuse and the continuing incest. I can understand why she did this. She believed it was her only hope. She thought, "If God cannot help me, maybe Satan will."

Notice how evil Satan is: he preys on the innocent victims. She was helpless—so the Evil One moved in on a helpless child, tempting her to make a pact with him in order to destroy her immortal soul. The Evil One is so sinister! So Sally said, "Satan, if you help me in this situation, if you give me control over my abusers, I will give you my life."

Things changed a little after that. The incest stopped, and Sally was able to survive her father's tantrums. She eventually left home at the age of eighteen. It seemed that Satan was going to fulfill his part of the bargain. He was simply waiting to wreak more destruction upon her.

About this time in her life Sally started to have thoughts of suicide. She knew this was wrong. Most of the time she was able to get rid of the thoughts easily, but sometimes they would linger. She would think, "Why don't I just jump out of my apartment window? Why don't I just drive my car into a wall?" But something always stopped her. I believe that Jesus heard her prayers to his mother. Because of her devotion to Mary, he intervened.

When Sally was twenty-two years old, she went to Medjugorje. There she had a powerful spiritual experience. For a while, things seemed to get better. Her life started to change. But when she returned, she went back to the lifestyle of the theater and immoral sexual relationships. All the thoughts of the past came back with force. The thoughts of suicide became more oppressive. Satan had not forgotten the pact she had made. Now he was ready to accept his reward for helping her.

But God had a different idea because she was a baptized Catholic. She would always be his adopted daughter. Even though Sally did not realize it, God had heard her prayers. Her devotion to Jesus' mother and the prayer support of others was about to change everything and set her on a path of freedom from satanic bondage and healing.

NINE

Our Weapons
for Battle

I met Sally for the first time on a Thursday afternoon. We began our meeting with a prayer, then she began to tell me about her childhood. She told me about the incest and her father's alcoholism and abuse. Sally did not believe that her mother loved her because she did not protect her but allowed the abuse to continue. She was afraid and ashamed, and felt hopeless.

As she was speaking I began to pray, asking the Lord what he wanted me to do. I just listened to her and to the Lord. Her life was so full of pain, and her story was overwhelming. But the key was that she wanted help. She did not want to commit suicide; she desired peace and freedom.

As I prayed I felt that something was not right. There was something else—other than what she told me—that needed to be dealt with before we could continue with counseling and inner healing. I finally asked her, "Did you ever make an agreement with Satan?" She remembered making that pact with him when she was twelve years old. Once she shared that with me I knew that we first had to break the satanic bondage before we could proceed.

I led her through a prayer of renunciation where she specifically renounced the pact with Satan saying, "In the name of Jesus I renounce my saying 'Satan, if you help me in this situation, if you give me control over my abusers, I will give you my life.'" Her head began to hurt and she felt nauseous. I then prayed a formal prayer, breaking all bondage to Satan and claiming her anew in the name of Jesus, through the power of his Blood. The bondage was broken and she was free.

But that was only the beginning of the work. We still needed to deal with the incest, her abusive father, and all the other issues of her childhood. In our counseling sessions we began to work on the emotional and psychological root causes of her problems. At the same time we changed the physical causes of her unhealthy diet and lack of exercise and motivation. We worked on the sin pattern of her life and helped her to build a relationship with Jesus Christ.

Finally, after five years of counseling and inner healing, she is able to live a normal and healthy life. She has a beautiful relationship with Jesus and Mary. She has steady employment; she is involved in the first healthy male-female relationship in her life. In examining her life story, we see the problems of her life were multidimensional, and there was a demonic infestation which had to be dealt with first. If the pact with Satan had not been broken she would never have been healed. But it would have been hazardous to stop only with the freedom from the bondage of Satan. She clearly needed counseling and inner healing.

In spiritual warfare we must use proper discernment and all the weapons God has given us. The human weapons we use are psychology, common sense, taking care of ourselves physically, and mutual support of one another. But what are our spiritual weapons that we use to oppose Satan and his machinations in our lives?

RENOUNCING THE OCCULT

The call of a follower of Jesus Christ is to "be holy, because I, the Lord your God, am holy" (Lv 19:2). Holiness is following the will of God and growing in his love. Walking in holiness is living in daily union with God. People have true happiness and joy when they are living in union with their Creator. "For the kingdom of God is not a matter of eating and drinking, but of righteousness, peace and joy in the Holy Spirit" (Rom 14:17). But sometimes the striving for union with God gets misdirected. This is what happens when someone becomes involved in the occult.

What is the occult? It is the realm of darkness, the things that bring an attachment to Satan and demonic spirits. There are three areas of the occult—divination, witchcraft, and sorcery. Divination is a pseudo-science of predicting future events or exploring past events through occult means.[1]

Such diviners are seeking knowledge that is not attainable through human or godly means. Knowledge comes either from God, human beings, or Satan. In divination, who is one asking for knowledge? Satan? God? Or human beings? (For a further explanation of the occult, refer to my book *Satanism: Is It Real?*). The answer is Satan in the case of traditional witchcraft.

When we talk about witchcraft as part of the occult we must make a distinction between witchcraft in the traditional sense of the word and modern witchcraft (also called Wicca). In performing traditional witchcraft, people hope to gain mastery of others and the world around them through spells and curses.[2]

Sorcery can be practiced by anyone who acquires the necessary magical substances and spells. In sorcery, a person is trying to influence human or natural events through an external force to effect a "magical result." This force, though invisible, is real.

Sorcery works through things. For example, music, charms, talismans, amulets, certain incantations, pieces of clothing, drugs, special rites, and images can be used in sorcery.[3]

Traditional witchcraft and sorcery imply a belief in an invisible reality. Their use brings one into bondage with that invisible reality. That invisible reality is not God, but an evil entity. In Christianity this evil entity is named Satan.

Wicca is a return to pagan nature religions. People who practice Wicca believe that by attuning themselves to the goddess Wicca, they can use magic spells to achieve their desires. Even though Wicca is not considered part of the occult *per se*, it involves the practice of occult methods of divination, astrology, and psychic power.

Through deception, Satan robs people of the joy found in union with God, for he is the Father of Lies. Liar that he is, Satan promises happiness, but he cannot deliver. Those who follow Satan will have happiness only when they escape his traps and commit their lives to Jesus Christ.

To be free from the ties to Satan, a person must renounce the occult. This renunciation should be spoken three times—once for each aspect of the demonic trinity. The person's *specific activity* in the occult should be part of the renunciation.

A Christian can break this bondage through the power of the name of Jesus. Christ gave authority to those who follow him (Lk 10). Through his death and resurrection Jesus destroyed the power of Satan but Satan continues to wage guerrilla warfare against Christians. However, that is all Satan can do. He cannot win the battle. Jesus has already done that! Satan trembles when Christians use the name of Jesus. Satan must obey the command of Christians when they use Jesus' holy name.

A qualifier is in order here. There are many approaches to leading those who were once involved in the occult in a prayer of renunciation. No single approach among those who minister is necessarily better than all the others. In this vein, what follows is a simple prayer of renunciation that the Lord has led me to use in helping people to renounce their involvement in the occult.

In the name of Jesus Christ, Son of the Living God, I renounce my involvement in (mention specific area of occult: ouija board, tarot cards, séances, Silva mind control, witchcraft, etc.). *Pray this prayer of renunciation three times.* (If a satanic pact has been entered into, renounce the promise you made to Satan word for word three times.)

I now invite you, Jesus, into my life. I give you, Jesus, my heart, my mind, my soul, and my strength. I accept you as my only Lord. I accept you as my only savior. I ask you, Jesus, to send me the Holy Spirit.

I invite you, Holy Spirit, into my life. Holy Spirit, fill me with your presence from the crown of my head to the soles of my feet. Place within me a desire for union with God, my Father. And I ask you, Holy Spirit, to give me the gift of prayer. Amen.

What I provide here is only some basic information on renunciation of the occult. For a more in-depth treatment, one can read *Deliverance from Evil Spirits: A Weapon for Spiritual Warfare* by Fr. Michael Scanlan and Randall Cirner (Servant Publications, 1980).

People give part of their mind and will to Satan through participation in the occult. These people must claim their mind and will back for the glory of God. They must let Satan know, beyond a shadow of a doubt, that he is not welcome in their lives. If they do not do so, something worse may happen to them. They must now turn their lives over to Jesus Christ.

When an evil spirit comes out of a man, it goes through arid places seeking rest and does not find it. Then it says, "I will return to the house I left." When it arrives, it finds the house unoccupied, swept clean and put in order. Then it goes and takes with it seven other spirits more wicked than itself, and they go in and live there. And the final condition of that man is worse than the first. That is how it will be with this wicked generation. Matthew 12:43-45

To stay free from harm, people who have been deeply involved in Satanism must follow the Lord Jesus. The spiritual pressure from the darkness can be great enough to disintegrate their personality. Only the light of Jesus Christ can stop it, bringing healing and peace.

Of course, the best medicine is preventive medicine. We take care of ourselves by using a proper balance of nutrition, exercise, and rest so we stay healthy. We must also take care of our spiritual life so that we stay spiritually healthy. Growing in holiness is preventive medicine against Satan and his deceptions. It is the work of all Christians. This is not easy. It takes discipline and hard work.

For our struggle is not against flesh and blood, but against the rulers, against the authorities, against the powers of this dark world and against the spiritual forces of evil in the heavenly realms. Therefore put on the full armor of God, so that when the day of evil comes, you may be able to stand your ground, and after you have done everything, to stand. Stand firm then, with the belt of truth buckled around your waist, with the breastplate of righteousness in place, and with your feet fitted with the readiness that comes from the gospel of peace. In addition to all this, take up the shield of faith, with which you can extinguish all the flaming arrows of the evil one. Take the helmet of salvation and the sword of the Spirit, which is the word of God. And pray in the Spirit on all occasions with all kinds of prayers and requests. With this in mind, be alert and always keep on praying for all the saints. Ephesians 6:12-18

THE ARMOR OF GOD

As one reads this passage it is important to pause and reflect upon each part of the armor. To place the belt of truth upon oneself means to live in the truth of Jesus Christ. What is that truth? Jesus is Lord and there is no other God. Jesus loves me and accepts me. He gave his life for me and he forgives me all my sins.

To place the breastplate of justice upon oneself means to live in the justice of God. Living in the justice of God is possible only when one is following the will of God. This takes discipline and resisting the desire to live in one's own sense of righteousness. We are to bring every decision we make to God.

If we make the choice to live in God's will, we will have happiness. When we come before God and say, "I only want to do your will, whatever you wish me to do, I will do," only then will we be truly free. We will be free from all oppression, anger, and fear. Sometimes we may be tempted to doubt God, but when we renounce that doubt and ask for faith to continue to believe, we will experience peace. Remember, God desires our happiness. He knows what is best for us, for he is our loving Father. "God is love. Whoever lives in love lives in God, and God in him" (1 Jn 4:16).

To place the gospel of peace upon oneself as footgear is to be the peace of Christ to all one meets. As Christians we are to represent the love of God to the world. Our actions and words spread this love.

To take up the shield of faith and ward off the fiery darts of Satan means to believe in the power of God. Satan, the Father of Lies, will hurl doubts about God's love at us. The shield of faith blocks these doubts. It assists us in remembering God's promises.

To place the helmet of salvation upon oneself is to protect

one's thoughts. Second Corinthians 10:5 encourages Christians to: "take captive every thought to make it obedient to Christ." This is essential because the mind is a vital battleground, and Satan wants to control it. Satan wants people to freely choose him. He tries to lead people into his kingdom of darkness through tempting thoughts. The helmet of salvation helps us to follow the Lord instead. We must claim our minds and emotions for the glory of God. Our every thought is to be purified by being made captive to Christ.

To take up the sword of the Spirit is to read and meditate upon the Word of God. It does no good to have a Bible in a house unless it is read. The Bible is God's word to his people. We need to reflect upon it every day in order to grow in holiness. As the Lord's people, we will know him when we meet him in the Scriptures and reflect upon his Word.

Along with placing the armor of God upon oneself every day, each of us should ask Jesus to cover ourselves and our families with his precious Blood. Along with this covering, we should ask for the protection of the mantel of Mary, the mother of Jesus and our spiritual mother. Asking for the intercession of the angels and saints also helps in protecting one from Satan's attacks, especially our guardian angel and saints with which we share a special relationship.

MARY

Chapter eight discussed some psychological problems that people have due to their family upbringing. Sometimes when we feel rejected by a parent that rejection can stay with us the rest of our lives. Mary can be a source of great healing for us if we have been rejected by our mother. A young woman came to me who was abused by her mother. As we prayed, I asked Jesus to allow Mary his mother to hold her. Tears started to well up in her eyes. She said that she had never experienced a mother's love until that moment. Jesus allowed Mary to fill her with a mother's love. Remember—Jesus gave Mary to us as a mother, and she loves us with a mother's love.

I also have prayed with men who have felt a great lack of a mother's love in their lives. When this happens to a man, he will either be very dependent on women or emotionally distant with them. After asking Mary to hold them in her arms and fill them with a mother's love, a dramatic change occurs in their lives. They are able to have better relationships with women. Through the intercession of Mary, their mother, these men have experienced healing.

If we have experienced that loss of a mother through death or divorce, or if we felt abandoned by our mother for any reason, we can pray to Mary. We can ask her to hold us and let us experience her maternal love. As we open ourselves to that outpouring, our lives will change. Mary's love will heal the mother wound, and we will experience the depths of our spiritual mother's love for us.

The rosary is especially dedicated to Mary and her intercession. It focuses on the joyful, sorrowful, and glorious mysteries of salvation, following the life of Jesus and Mary. It comes to us from the Middle Ages where it became a substitute for the recitation of the Divine Office because some monks in the monasteries and most of the laity did not know how to read. Instead of the one hundred fifty psalms, they would recite one hundred fifty "Our Fathers" which they counted off on a ring of beads.[4] With the popularity of Marian devotion in the twelfth century, the monks established a *Psalter of the Blessed Virgin* which consisted of one hundred fifty Hail Marys. Gradually the *Psalter of the Blessed Virgin* became more popular than the *Psalter of the Father*.

Later the one hundred fifty Hail Marys were divided into fifteen decades, separated by reciting one Our Father.[5] In the fifteenth century the Dominicans had established the rosary in its present form. In the early 1500s the rosary became a symbol of the Catholic faith and a powerful weapon for spiritual warfare. Pope St. Pius V established October 7 as the Feast of the Most Holy Rosary, in thanksgiving for the victory of Lepanto, which marked a turning point in Christian Europe halting the advance of Islam.

There are many different ways to pray the rosary. We can meditate on each mystery as we pray the rosary. We may wish to add different scriptural meditations. We do not have to use only the mysteries that are traditionally used. In the 1400s there were three hundred different mysteries used to meditate on all of salvation history. I myself have just started uniting the prayer of tongues (1 Cor 12:10) and the rosary. I pray in tongues for a couple of minutes between each decade of the rosary; I find this method a very powerful prayer of intercession.

Whatever your approach with devotion to Mary, recognize God's great gift in her of a mother for you. Avail yourself of her powerful intercession, particularly when you're sorely tempted.

THE SAINTS

In some difficulties, we need more than just information and input from friends. We need the support of other people's prayers. Whenever I have a difficult decision to make, I always ask people to pray for me. The people I ask to pray for me are Christians who are alive in this world and the saints who are alive with Christ in heaven.

In addition to Mary as our spiritual mother, we ask the saints to pray for us when we say a novena or other prayer to a saint. In these prayers we are asking for this saint's intercession. A novena is a special prayer that a person prays for nine days. These nine days of prayer are offered for a special intention, asking for the saint's intercession. The first novena prayed by the church was to the Holy Spirit when the apostles were gathered in the upper room for nine days, waiting for the Holy Spirit to fall upon them (Acts 1:14).

We have special gifts from God. "God has appointed first of all apostles, second prophets, third teachers, then workers of miracles, also those having gifts of healing, those able to help others, those with gifts of administration, and those speaking in different kinds of tongues" (1 Cor 12:27-28). The Holy Spirit empowers us with various gifts to use for the growth of the church. The saints also have special gifts for our community. In fact, many of them have been assigned as patrons and patronesses to assist us in particular vocations, occupations, or in times of need.

Do I feel that I am in a hopeless situation? Then I can ask for St. Jude's intercession or even pray a novena to him. Cancer? I ask for St. Peregrine's help. Have I lost something? I ask for St. Anthony's prayers to find what I lost. Am I experiencing problems in a pregnancy or childbirth? I ask St. Gerard Majella for prayers. A close friend of mine had trouble with the birth of her three children. When she became pregnant a fourth time, she started to ask for St. Gerard Majella's assistance. Through this intercessory prayer she had no problems with her fourth birth. Many church choirs invoke the help of St. Cecilia, asking for her prayers that they may be able to sing the praises of God, because she is the patroness of music. People with eye problems are encouraged to ask for the intercession of St. Lucy.

One of my favorite saints is St. Benedict. He was an exorcist in the early church. A religious sister I know was having problems with her car. She had an extremely strange series of auto accidents. She was not hitting other people's cars but they were crashing into hers. I blessed a medal of St. Benedict for her. She placed it in her car and has not had an accident since.

Reading the lives of the saints can be spiritually uplifting for us. When we read their lives, we discover the struggles that they had in following God. Sometimes their difficulties are similar to our own. When we discover a saint who had similar problems to ours, we can ask that saint to intercede for us. We ask him or her to pray that God will give us the same grace to overcome a similar difficulty. In this way, the saints can become our lifelong helpers and our models on our journey to heaven.

We also have special saints. They are called our name saints. Remember, in baptism we received a saint's name. This saint is to be our special intercessor before God's throne. In the sacrament of confirmation, we chose a saint that exemplified a virtue or a lifestyle that we wished to follow in our lives. This saint also is a special intercessor. I have four saints as special intercessors because my first, middle, and last names are the names of saints. And for my confirmation name, I chose St. Damian, a simple farmer who evangelized the Polish people. These saints can be very helpful to us in spiritual warfare because we share a spiritual family bond with them when we share their names. They are great intercessors in heaven for us.

THE ANGELS

Along with the saints, I believe God wishes to use his angels to help us in our daily struggle. The angels minister to us (Heb 1:14). As we have seen in the Bible, God sent his angels to assist people in answer to their prayers (see chapter five). The angels announced the message of Jesus' birth to the shepherds and the whole world. The Father comforted Jesus with his angels after Jesus' fast of forty days in the desert. An angel strengthened Jesus in the Garden of Gethsemane.

God desires to continue sending his angels. They can assist us in our struggle against the powers of the Evil One. For instance, St. Michael is our spiritual warrior since he fought against Satan and the demonic spirits (Rv 12:7-9). I believe that I have been protected from harm through the ministry of angels. I cannot begin to count the number of "close calls" I have had while driving to give a teaching on the occult or some other aspect of our faith.

On a Thursday evening I was driving to give a talk on spiritual warfare at an area church. I was on the freeway, driving the speed limit. I had just finished praying my rosary and was listening to some Christian music. Suddenly, two cars sped by me, changing lanes and weaving in and out of traffic. In order to avoid them, another car swerved right in front of me. I don't know how I missed hitting that car.

Another evening I was driving to Pomona to give a talk on the occult. I was at a stop sign in Pomona when a car turned the corner going over fifty miles an hour with a police car in hot pursuit. I asked St. Michael to surround my car with his angels. Both cars just barely missed hitting me.

Some people have even had experiences of someone showing up out of nowhere to help them in a time of need. They never see the person again. Are these helpers angels sent by God? The book of Tobit tells the story of one such instance. God sent the archangel Raphael to help Tobit and Tobiah in the form of a kinsman.

In my prayer I have asked God to send forth his angels to do his will. As I prepare for Sunday Mass, I ask the Lord to send his angels to the northern, southern, eastern, and western boundaries of my parish to draw God's people to church. I ask the angels to bind the workings of any evil spirit in the lives of the parishioners so that they may come here and receive the blessings of God.

We can pray the same prayer for our respective parishes. We can ask God to send his angels forth to call his people to worship. We can ask for the angels to assist the priest when he preaches. Remember that an angel touched the mouth of Isaiah with burning coal to purify his lips to proclaim God's message (Is 6:6-7). We also can ask the angels to protect our spouse, children, extended family members, and possessions. Whenever I leave my car I ask the Lord to send an angel to watch over my car and the possessions inside it.

If I am interceding for one person in particular, I will ask God to send St. Michael the archangel to remove any demonic oppression in the person's life. I then ask God to send St. Raphael the archangel to heal the person. I ask for St. Raphael's intercession because the book of Tobit recounts God's sending the angel Raphael to heal Tobit and free Sarah, his bride, from demonic oppression. Raphael's intercession is also asked before long journeys because he traveled with Tobit's son Tobiah. The name Raphael means "God heals."

If someone needs instruction in the Word of God, I ask God to send St. Gabriel the archangel to instruct the person. I ask the intercession of St. Gabriel because he is a special messenger from God. Gabriel announced the message to Mary that she was to be the mother of Jesus (Lk 1:26-37). Gabriel was also sent to the prophet Daniel to give him understanding and an answer to his prayer (Dn 9:20-23).

I also ask that the person's guardian angel will be empowered in a special way to give him or her knowledge of God and strength to follow the commandments.

These prayers are effectual. As we continue to intercede for a person in this way, a change gradually happens in his or her life. Another powerful prayer asking for the assistance of the angels is the chaplet of St. Michael, which also invokes the aid of various choirs of angels with specific ministries.

The Chaplet of St. Michael the Archangel.

O God, come to my assistance.
   O Lord, make haste to help me. Glory be to the Father, etc.
   First Salutation: One Our Father and three Hail Marys in

honor of the first choir of angels. By the intercession of St. Michael and the celestial choir of seraphim, may the Lord make us worthy to burn with the fire of perfect charity. Amen.

Second Salutation: One Our Father and three Hail Marys in honor of the second choir of angels. By the intercession of St. Michael and the celestial choir of cherubim, may the Lord vouchsafe to grant us grace to leave the ways of wickedness and run in the paths of Christian perfection. Amen.

Third Salutation: One Our Father and three Hail Marys in honor of the third choir of angels. By the intercession of St. Michael and the celestial choir of thrones, may the Lord infuse into our hearts a true and sincere spirit of humility. Amen.

Fourth Salutation: One Our Father and three Hail Marys in honor of the fourth choir of angels. By the intercession of St. Michael and the celestial choir of dominions, may the Lord give us grace to govern our senses and subdue our unruly passions. Amen.

Fifth Salutation: One Our Father and three Hail Marys in honor of the fifth choir of angels. By the intercession of St. Michael and the celestial choir of powers, may the Lord vouchsafe to protect our souls against the snares and temptation of the devil. Amen.

Sixth Salutation: One Our Father and three Hail Marys in honor of the sixth choir of angels. By the intercession of St. Michael and the celestial choir of virtues, may the Lord preserve us from evil, and suffer us not to fall into temptation. Amen.

Seventh Salutation: One Our Father and three Hail Marys in honor of the seventh choir of angels. By the intercession of St. Michael and the celestial choir of principalities, may God fill our souls with a true spirit of obedience. Amen.

Eighth Salutation: One Our Father and three Hail Marys in honor of the eighth choir of angels. By the intercession of St. Michael and the celestial choir of archangels, may the Lord give us perseverance in faith and in all good works, in order that we *gain the glory of Paradise. Amen.*

Ninth Salutation: One Our Father and three Hail Marys in honor of the ninth choir of angels. By the intercession of St. Michael and the celestial choir of angels, may the Lord grant us to be protected by our mortal life and conducted hereafter to eternal glory. Amen.

At the end say four Our Fathers.

The first in honor of St. Michael,
The second in honor of St. Gabriel,
The third in honor of St. Raphael,
The fourth in honor of our guardian angel.

Then say the following invocation:

O glorious prince St. Michael, chief and commander of the heavenly hosts, guardian of souls, vanquisher of rebel spirits, servant in the house of the divine king, and our admirable conductor, thou who dost shine with excellence and superhuman virtue, vouchsafe to deliver us from evil, who turn to thee with confidence, and enable us by thy gracious protection to serve God more and more faithfully every day. Pray for us, O glorious St. Michael, prince of the church of Jesus Christ. That we may be made worthy of his promises. Amen.

Almighty and everlasting God,
Who by a prodigy of goodness and a merciful desire for the salvation of all men, hast appointed the most glorious archangel St. Michael, prince of thy church, make us worthy, we beseech thee, to be delivered by his powerful protection from all our enemies, that none of them may harass us at the hour of death, but that we may be conducted by him into the august presence of thy divine majesty. This we beg through the merits of Jesus Christ our Lord. Amen.

Our Guardian Angel. In chapter five, I included the prayer to our guardian angel. God gives us a special helper whom we call our guardian angel. God in his great love for us gives us an angel to help us in the spiritual battle. This angel daily intercedes for us before the throne of God (Mt 18:10). He carries our prayers to God's throne for us. This angel is given to us at the beginning of our lives. God does not force our guardian angel upon us. It is up to us to ask for his help and his intercession.

He can help us live a virtuous life and understand God's Word. He will not leave us. He is always there in our hour of need. Even if we commit mortal sin, our guardian angel will not leave our side. He will pray for us and wait until we return to God. And when we do repent, he will rejoice (Lk 15:10).

Our guardian angel never wishes to divert our eyes away from God. His desire is solely that we be faithful to God. To blatantly refuse our guardian angel's help is to say that we do not need his assistance, that we can handle things by ourselves. But if God created these angels to guard and protect us throughout our lives, he in his wisdom knows that we need their assistance.

Our guardian angel is especially important in spiritual warfare. He can help us fight off the temptations of Satan, who is himself a fallen angel. So, too, when we ask our angel for help in times of confusion, he will instruct us in God's wisdom. When we ask for help in difficulties, he will give us strength. When we are weak, he will help to make us strong.

In calling upon your guardian angel, you may want to make the following prayer your own:

Holy guardian angel, you who have been given to me by God as my companion throughout my life, save me for eternity and fulfill in me your duty given to you by the Love of God. Shake off my indifference, strengthen me in my weakness, block for

*me every wrong way, open my eyes to God and the Cross, but
close my ears to the prompting of the wicked adversary. Watch
over me when I sleep and let me one day be your joy and your
reward in heaven. Amen.*[6]

THE ARMOR OF PRAYER

Growing in holiness means growing in daily prayer. A person
seeking holiness should strive for a vibrant prayer life. Prayer
can take many forms: praying in one's home (whether the
prayers are devotional or spontaneous), listening to Christian
music, reading and reflecting on the Bible, or celebrating at
church services.

Sometimes it seems difficult to find the time to pray. As
mentioned earlier, Fr. Michael Scanlan suggests making an
appointment with God each day and writing it in your daily
schedule. If a day is so programmed that there is no time for
prayer, the solution is simple: get up earlier.

Every morning I pray the following, which was composed by
Sister Betty Igo and myself on a trip to Medjugorje. (Part of
this prayer is contained in Fr. Robert DeGrandis' book,
Intergenerational Healing.) First, imagine, think, or feel your
family under the cross, covered with his light and precious
Blood, then pray:

*I welcome the power of the resurrected Christ in any stronghold
Satan thinks he may have in or around me, and in the name of
Jesus I break any generational or personal hold of the spirits
that torment me or my generations.*

*I place upon myself the helmet of salvation, the breastplate of
righteousness, the belt of truth, and the shoes of the gospel of
peace. I take up the shield of faith and the sword of the Spirit,
the Word of God.*

In the name of Jesus Christ and by my authority as a

Christian, I bind you, Satan, and all demonic spirits on the earth, in the air, in the fire, in the water, in the atmosphere, in the netherworld, and all the satanic forces of nature. I bind you from any intercommunication or interrelationship with each other. I separate you totally and completely from each other.

(pray the following paragraph three times)

In the name of the Father, the Son, and the Holy Spirit, I rebuke and bind any spirit not of our Lord Jesus Christ and I command it to leave my presence, possessions, and loved ones. I bind and break every satanic sacrifice, curse, hex, seal, spell, sorcery, and anything else of like nature, also any disease placed upon me or my family by any agent or brought upon us by our own mistakes or sins.

In the name of Jesus Christ I bind all spirits of the north, south, east, and west, and all other evil spirits trying to influence the personnel, functions, and property of my parish. Lord God, send your angels into these regions to draw your people to you.

Mary the Immaculate, clothe me in the light, power, and energy of your faith. Father, please assign angels and saints to assist me. I ask that my guardian angel will protect me from sin. Thank you Jesus for being my wisdom, my justice, my sanctification and my redemption. I surrender to the ministry of the Holy Spirit.

Glory be to the Father, to the Son, and to the Holy Spirit. As it was in the beginning, is now and ever shall be. Amen.

Saint Michael, the archangel defend us in the battle. Be our protection against the wickedness and snares of the devil. May God rebuke him, we humbly pray, and do thou, O prince of the heavenly host, by the power of God, thrust into hell Satan and all evil spirits who wander through the world for the ruin of souls. Amen.

Deliverance prayer. In addition to regular daily prayer, deliverance prayer is one of the oldest traditions of the Catholic Church. In the Our Father we pray, "Deliver us from evil." That prayer is a prayer for deliverance. Christians are able to pray for deliverance from evil spirits because Jesus gave them that power. In Luke 10, Jesus commissioned the seventy-two to spread the kingdom of God. In this action Jesus gave them authority over demonic spirits. The seventy-two, upon their return to Jesus, exclaimed, "Even the demons are subject to us in your name!"

Deliverance prayer is not solemn exorcism. There are two forms of exorcism: solemn exorcism and private exorcism. Solemn exorcism is a liturgical rite of the Catholic Church. It is a public action of the church. Solemn exorcism can only be performed by an official delegate of the Bishop.

Private exorcism is not a public, liturgical rite of the church. The terms of private exorcism (also called simple exorcism) and deliverance refer to the same action. This style of prayer is used to curb the influence of Satan in the lives of Christians. Whereas in solemn exorcism only the delegate of the Bishop may perform the exorcism, any Christian can pray deliverance prayer.

Deliverance prayer is prayed in the name of Jesus. Solemn exorcism is prayed in the name of Jesus and the whole church. It would seem logical that a priest, by the power of the sacrament of holy orders, has a greater commission than the laity to pray deliverance prayer. This is not always the case because this prayer is a charism. God can give charisms to whomever he chooses. Even so, there are certain guidelines that are to be followed in this type of prayer.

In 1986, in response to some questionable activities, the Sacred Congregation for the Doctrine of Faith published the following statement:

1. Canon 1172 of the Canonical Code declares that nobody can legitimately perform exorcisms on possessed persons, unless he obtains a special and appropriate permission from the territorial Bishop, and determines that this permission be given by the territorial Bishop only to a priest endowed with piety, knowledge, prudence, and integrity of life. The Bishops, therefore, are earnestly asked to demand the observance of these rules.

2. It follows from these rules, that even the faithful may not be allowed to make use of the formula of exorcism against Satan and his fallen angels, taken from the one that was made public by order of Pope Leo XIII, and much less to use the whole text of this exorcism. The Bishops ought to inform the faithful about this matter if the case demands.

3. Finally, for the same reasons, the Bishops are requested to watch that, even in cases where a true diabolical possession is excluded, those who lack the proper permission do not supervise or direct the assemblies in which prayers are used to obtain a releasing, in the course of which the devils are disturbed and their identities are sought. However, the declaration of these norms by no means should keep the faithful from praying to be delivered from evil, as Jesus taught. Moreover, the Bishops will be able to use any given opportunity to recall what the tradition of the Church teaches about the role played by the sacraments and the intervention of the Blessed Virgin Mary, of the Angels, and of the Saints in the spiritual struggle of the Christians against the evil spirits.

In examination of these norms, we must again stress that deliverance prayer is not solemn exorcism, which can be performed only by an authorized priest. This statement also does not mention silent exorcism. Silent exorcism can be a very powerful prayer. In the sacrament of reconciliation priests are encouraged to use silent exorcism when it will be beneficial to the penitent.

The following should be kept in mind with deliverance prayer. It should *never* be done in a large group setting. It is best that this prayer be prayed silently. Since the prayer of deliverance rests on the authority of Jesus, there is no need to shout. Shouting does not make Jesus any more powerful. The following is a schema for deliverance prayer.

1. Begin with praise and thanks to God.
2. Pray for the protection of everyone present and all family members.
3. Ask for the intercession of Mary, the angels (especially St. Michael), and the saints.
4. Bind the power of Satan and demonic spirits. The following is a simple binding prayer:

   In the name of Jesus Christ, Son of the living God, I bind you Satan, and all of your evil companions on the earth, in the air, in the fire, in the water, in the atmosphere, and all the Satanic forces of nature. In the name of Jesus, and by my authority as a Christian, I bind you from any intercommunication and interrelationship with each other. I separate you completely from each other. In the name of Jesus, I bind you from causing any disturbance, confusion, anxiety, or manifestation of any sort. In the name of Jesus, I command you to be completely silent.

5. Pray a deliverance prayer quietly. If a person has the charismatic gift of word of knowledge or discernment of spirits, he or she may know the name of a spirit, for example, "the spirit of fear." The prayer prayed silently would be: "In the name of Jesus, I command the spirit of fear to leave this person

immediately and go directly to the cross where Jesus will do with you as he wills."

6. After the deliverance prayer, pray that the Holy Spirit will come upon the person and bring him or her healing. Ask the Holy Spirit to fill the person with grace. This is a good opportunity to pray for inner healing.

Admittedly, this is only a brief outline of one possible approach to deliverance. For a more in-depth presentation on deliverance, please see *Deliverance from Evil Spirits,* by Fr. Michael Scanlan, T.O.R., and Randall Cirner, which was earlier recommended and is listed in the bibliography. They present a balanced and pastorally sensitive approach to deliverance that is faithful to Catholic teaching.

Communion, confession, and devotions. Frequent reception of Holy Communion and the sacrament of reconciliation is important in the regular prayer life of a Catholic. Jesus gave the apostles the power to forgive sins in his name when he said: "If you forgive anyone his sins, they are forgiven; if you do not forgive them, they are not forgiven" (Jn 20:23). The power to forgive sins in the name of Jesus has been passed down through the centuries by the sacrament of holy orders to the bishops and priests of today. Christians should confess their sins daily to the Lord and go to confession frequently.

The reception of Holy Communion is extremely important to a Catholic. The Eucharist is the Body and Blood of Jesus Christ. While it is good to ask for the protection of the Blood of Christ each day, it is better to ask for that protection during the Eucharistic celebration, when one receives the Body and Blood of Christ.

Throughout its history, the Catholic Church has emphasized the power of the Body and Blood of Christ. Miracles have demonstrated that the bread and wine are, in fact, changed into the Body and Blood of Christ. The bread and wine are not merely symbols of Jesus—they indeed become the Body and Blood of Christ.

Making the sign of the cross is a powerful prayer. Through it, Satan is confronted with the reality that he has been vanquished. Further, praying before a crucifix can be a great weapon against Satan, because it is through the cross that people receive redemption.

Christians should incorporate praise into their prayer life as well. Praying the psalms of praise can be a help. They aid us in lifting our hearts to the Lord. Praying in tongues can also be of great assistance. This gift, often experienced by Catholic Charismatics or Pentecostals, is a gift of the Holy Spirit (1 Cor 12:10). Paul says, "I thank God that I speak in tongues more than all of you" (1 Cor 14:18).

While praying in tongues comes from the Holy Spirit, it remains under the control of the person's will. This gift is the power of the Holy Spirit praying within the person. Modern praying in tongues was called jubilation in the early church.[7] Singing in tongues was a part of the liturgy of the church until the ninth century.[8] I encourage you to read *Sounds of Wonder* by Eddie Ensley for an excellent history and description of this gift, sometimes called praying in the Spirit. Ephesians 6:18 encourages the followers of God to pray in the Spirit.

Another element of a full prayer life is fasting. In fasting a person seeks the discipline of God to turn away from sin. A fast can be partial or total. A total fast is taking no solid food and drinking only water. One also can fast by not eating certain types of foods that one normally enjoys. When I fast, I turn to God and ask him how he wants me to fast and for how long I am to fast. This then becomes God's fast, not my fast.

Homes should be dedicated to the Lord. An excellent method of dedicating a home is the enthronement to the Sacred Heart of Jesus. In this enthronement, we ask Jesus to have full dominion in our home, to make his Holy Spirit reign in our family, and to give us strength to imitate the virtues of the Holy Family—Jesus, Mary, and Joseph.

If the house is not blessed, the priest blesses the house. Then the priest blesses the image of the Sacred Heart of Jesus. After this, the family prays the Apostle's Creed. Then they pray the following prayer of consecration:

O most Sacred Heart of Jesus, you revealed to St. Margaret Mary your desire to rule over Christian families; behold, in order to please you we gather before you this day to proclaim your full sovereignty over our family. We desire henceforth to live your life; we desire that the virtues, to which you have promised peace on earth, may flower in the bosom of our family; we desire to keep far from us the spirit of the world, which you have condemned. You are King of our minds by the simplicity of our faith; you are King of our hearts by our love for you alone with which our hearts are on fire, and whose flame we shall keep alive by frequently receiving the Holy Eucharist.

Be pleased, O Sacred Heart, to preside over our gathering together, to bless our spiritual and temporal affairs, to ward off all annoyance from us, to sanctify our joys and comfort our sorrows. If any of us has ever been so unhappy as to fall into the misery of displeasing you grant that he may remember, O Heart of Jesus, that you are full of goodness and mercy toward the repentant sinner. And when the hour of separation strikes and death enters our family circle, whether we go or whether we stay, we shall all bow humbly before your eternal decrees. This shall be our consolation, to remember that the day will come when our entire family, once more united in heaven, shall be able to sing of your glory and goodness forever. May the Immaculate Heart of Mary and the glorious patriarch St. Joseph deign to offer you our act of consecration, and to keep the memory of it alive in us all the days of our lives.

Glory to the Heart of Jesus, our King and our father!

Finally, the whole family recites:

We consecrate to you, O Heart of Jesus, the trials and joys and all the happiness of our family life, and we beg you to pour out your best blessings on all its members, present and absent, living and dead. And when one after the other we shall have closed our eyes in holy death, O Jesus, may all of us in Paradise find again our entire family, united in your Sacred Heart. Amen.

The priest closes with the following act of thanksgiving:

O good Jesus, we thank you for the most merciful love which you have showered today on this family. You chose it as your property and prepared in it a dwelling place, that with your love and providence you may protect and guide it. Grant to all its members abundant grace, so that they may obey you and preserve their faith.

Strengthen in us faith and charity. Make us meek and humble of heart, so that we may lead a pure and holy life according to your will. Let this home be another Nazareth, so that peace and charity may reign in it and keep all its members united till death.

May the Most Sacred Heart of Jesus and the Immaculate Heart of Mary be ever loved and honored in this home. Amen.

Religious articles and pictures, such as a crucifix and statues of the Madonna and Child, help to remind people to center their lives on God. One can also wear a crucifix or a medal, invoking the prayers of Jesus, Mary, or a saint. When people wear these religious articles, they should reflect upon their meaning and ask for the grace to follow God.

It is easier to live a Christian life if a person has friends who are following Christ. They can be a support in times of trouble. It also is wise to have a prayer partner with whom one prays on a regular basis. Joining a prayer group also fosters Christian fellowship.

Christian reading assists spiritual growth. It can be writings of the saints, the lives of the saints, books on prayer, or any work that draws one closer to God. Such study can educate one to discern what is not of God and help form one's conscience in the Lord.

Devotional prayers also help us in the spiritual battle. The following chaplets can give us great strength in time of trial.

CHAPLETS

The Chaplet of the Holy Spirit. This chaplet consists of five groups of seven beads each. Before and after each group, there are two large beads. In addition there are three small beads at the beginning. On these three beads, one makes the sign of the cross, recites an act of contrition, and sings the hymn "Come, Holy Ghost."

In each group, the Glory Be is said on the seven small beads, and one Our Father and one Hail Mary on the two large beads. On the last two large beads pray the Apostle's Creed, one Our Father, and one Hail Mary for the intention of the Holy Father.

There is a mystery for each group for reflection:

The First Mystery: By the Holy Spirit is Jesus conceived of the Blessed Virgin Mary.

The Second Mystery: The Spirit of the Lord rested upon Jesus.

The Third Mystery: By the Spirit is Jesus led into the desert.

The Fourth Mystery: The Holy Spirit in the Church (Pentecost).

The Fifth Mystery: The Holy Spirit in the soul of the just person.

The Chaplet of the Sacred Heart. The chaplet consists of five groups of beads, six small beads, and one large bead. To begin the chaplet make the sign of the cross and pray the Anima Christi:

> *Soul of Christ, sanctify me. Body of Christ, save me. Blood of Christ, inebriate me. Water from the side of Christ, wash me. Passion of Christ, strengthen me. O good Jesus, hear me. That with your saints I may be praising you forever and ever. Amen.*

On the large bead pray: *Sweetest heart of Jesus, I implore that I may love thee more and more.* On the six small beads pray: *Sweet heart of Jesus, be my love.* At end of the six beads pray: *Sweet heart of Mary, be my salvation.* On the large bead pray: *May the sweet heart of Jesus in the blessed sacrament be blessed, loved, and adored, in every tabernacle throughout the world at every moment until the end of time. Amen.*

The Chaplet of Mercy. This chaplet consists of five groups of ten small beads. Before the small bead of each group is one large bead. Begin the chaplet with one Our Father, one Hail Mary, and the Apostle's Creed. On the single bead pray: *Eternal Father, I offer you the Body and Blood, soul and divinity of your dearly beloved Son, our Lord Jesus Christ, in atonement for our sins and those of the whole world.* On the ten beads pray: *For the sake of his sorrowful passion, have mercy on us and on the whole world.* Closing prayer: (Pray three times) *Holy God, Holy Mighty One, Holy Immortal One, have mercy on us, and on the whole world. Amen.*

THE SACRAMENTS: GOD'S SPECIAL GIFTS

The Catholic Church celebrates seven special gifts from God. These are the seven sacraments: Baptism, confirmation, Holy

Eucharist, reconciliation, anointing of the sick, matrimony, and holy orders. Each sacrament has a special character and power for sanctification. We call this sacramental grace. We can call on the special sacramental graces to help us in our spiritual battle.

Paul tells Timothy, "For this reason I remind you to fan into flame the gift of God, which is in you through the laying on of my hands" (2 Tm 1:6). Timothy was encouraged to pray that God would inflame the gifts of his Sacrament that he received through the laying on of hands—holy orders. Through this new empowerment he would receive all that he needed to lead his community.

We can pray in the same way that Paul encouraged Timothy. We can ask God to inflame or stir up the graces that we received when we were baptized, confirmed, married, etc. As we examine the special character of the sacraments, we will know what grace is being empowered in us anew.

Baptism. In the Sacrament of Baptism we receive God's life. We are freed from original sin and given a proper orientation toward God. We receive gifts of faith, hope and love. John made an appointment to see me because he had been involved in the occult. He had used ouija boards, attended séances, and went to psychic healers. I was going to lead John through a prayer of renunciation, but God did not want me to do that.

Instead, God wanted me to see the power of invoking the sacramental grace of Baptism. I prayed, "Father, I ask you to fan into flame the gifts that John received at his Baptism. May the baptismal graces come to a new fullness in his life." As I prayed John's head began to turn from side to side. He felt pressure in his head. Finally the manifestation of the pain stopped. He looked at me and told me he felt something depart when I prayed that prayer.

We can pray this prayer when we are experiencing doubt or fear. Ask God to fan into flame the baptismal graces. If a child has fallen away from the church, the parents can ask God to renew the graces and gifts of Baptism. I know of three people who have returned to active participation in the church as a result of this prayer.

Confirmation. We can ask God to fan into flame the graces of confirmation. We can ask him for a fresh outpouring of these graces in our lives. This will give us a new strength to operate in the gifts of the Holy Spirit and to grow in the fruit of the Spirit. We will be strengthened to be witnesses to Jesus Christ.

Matrimony. The special character of matrimony is a grace of unity for the married couple and the gifts necessary to care for their family. Couples can ask God to renew these graces in their lives, especially in times of marital difficulty and on anniversaries. When they pray in this way, the problems of everyday life are less burdensome. There is greater peace in the family.

Anointing the Sick. The sacrament of anointing of the sick is administered to those in need of healing. I believe this sacrament can be used not only for physical sickness, but also for healing of mental, emotional, and spiritual sickness. When we ask God to fan into flame this sacramental grace, we receive healing where we need it the most in our lives. Through the continual asking of God to inflame this grace, we will grow in health.

Holy Orders. In holy orders a person is set aside to teach, govern, and sanctify the people of God. Many priests have experienced a renewed gift of preaching when they prayed that God would fan into flame the graces of their ordination. The people of a parish can ask God to do this for their pastors.

Reconciliation. The grace of the sacrament of reconciliation helps us to change our lives. We are not perfect; we sin. In the prayer of the absolution, we receive forgiveness of our sins and a sacramental grace for change. If I have a habitual sin in my life, I can ask God to fan the flame of this sacramental grace into conversion, so I can turn away from this sin and be faithful to Jesus' call. For example, if I have a problem with lust or pornography, I can ask God to fan into flame the grace of reconciliation. This will strengthen me to let go of the pornography and avoid occasions of sin. I can pray this prayer for any sinful area of my life.

Holy Eucharist and the power of the Mass. The special grace of the Eucharist is union with God and each other as the body of Christ. In a sense, the Eucharist encompasses all the sacramental graces. In the Mass there is forgiveness with the penitential rite, prayers for healing in the petitions, teachings through the Word of God and preaching, special graces in the prayers and blessings of the Mass, and new empowerment for union with God and one another in Holy Communion.

I believe that we can receive powerful healing when we learn how to pray the Mass for healing. In his book, *Healing through the Mass*, Fr. Robert DeGrandis teaches how to pray the Mass in this special way. The following is not meant to be a synopsis of his book. I simply highlight a couple of his points and add some personal thoughts and prayers to help if you wish to know how to pray the Mass in this way.

The Mass surpasses all other sacramental activities in holiness because it is an action of Christ the priest and his body which is the church. It is the summit toward which the activity of the church is directed and the font from which all her power flows. It is a source of grace and moves us to unity and love. But in order for the Mass to be effective in our lives, we must realize what we are doing. We need to be properly disposed. And we must participate in the Mass.

To fully participate in the Mass, we must have a daily prayer life, reflecting on the Word of God. If we do not have a daily prayer life, then our celebration of the Mass will not become what it is meant to be for each one of us. There are three tripods to prayer: communal (the Mass), small group or family prayer, and individual prayer.

Bishop Fulton Sheen said that the church could be renewed if everyone would spend twenty minutes a day in mental prayer, which includes scripture reading and meditation time. Pope Pius XII said that liturgical prayer nourishes private prayer, and private prayer nourishes liturgical prayer. Praying the Mass for healing then begins at home with private prayer. The private prayer of the community during the week empowers the prayer of the assembled community at Mass.

The Sign of the Cross. The Mass begins with the sign of the cross, an expression of our faith that we are gathered in the name of the Trinity. We begin in the name of the Father—our loving Father who is merciful, loves us, and sent us Jesus to heal us. In the very beginning of Mass, or the moment that we walk into the church, we sign ourselves with the sign of the cross. In this action we could ask for healing of any negative attitudes which we have developed through the years toward God as a loving Father.

Reasons why we may not have a proper idea of God as a loving Father could be due to personal sufferings, sickness, or a poor, unloving relationship with our earthly father. These can affect one's attitude toward God as our heavenly Father. Some people have an unconscious fear of God, believing that if you love the Lord and get to close to him, he will make you suffer—that somehow your happiness will diminish. These thoughts perpetuate fear and are inconsistent with the idea of God as a loving Father. We pray: *In the name of the Father who sent Jesus to heal us; in the name of the Son, Jesus the Healer, our*

Redeemer, and in the name of the Holy Spirit who empowers us to do the work of Jesus in the world. Amen.

Penitential Rite. Forgiveness is primary in our healing process. Do I really believe that the Father forgives me for all the wrong that I have done? In the penitential rite we open ourselves to receive the forgiveness of the Lord, and we reach out in forgiveness of one another and of ourselves. Unforgiveness can block the healing power of God's love in our lives. Unforgiveness can cause different physical, psychological, emotional, and spiritual problems.

We need to extend forgiveness to ourselves and others, and to let go of resentments that we may have against God, because of hurts, pains, death of a loved one, or unanswered prayers. We also need to forgive the church. Many of us have been hurt by certain people in the church. At this time of the Mass we can center on one person or a number of people we need to forgive. If you cannot think of anyone, pray and ask the Holy Spirit to reveal that person to you.

The Collect or Opening Prayer. The "Let us pray" is the invitation by the priest to the community to enter into the opening prayer of the Mass. In the past this was called the "Collect." The people are to bring their private themes or petitions to the Lord as the priest unites all the prayers of the people in the opening prayer, presenting them to the Lord. There is power in this community prayer before the Blessed Sacrament, especially when the people present have been praying during the week.

The Creed or *Profession of Faith.* In the Creed, as a people of God, we make a new commitment to our Lord Jesus Christ. We publicly proclaim that we accept Jesus and his teachings.

The creed is a summary and renewal of our faith and belief in Jesus Christ and all that he has taught us. If we call our entrance song a kind of national anthem of our faith, and the sign of the cross a sort of salute to God, then we can call the Profession of Faith our pledge of allegiance. After the Creed, we intercede for our needs, both personal and those of our brothers and sisters.

The Offertory. As the bread and wine are brought forward at the offertory, we can bring ourselves, broken, in need of healing, to the Lord. Now is an excellent time to offer to God one of our petitions in which we seek healing. We can place our own brokenness or that of loved ones or friends—whether it be physical, psychological, emotional, or spiritual—upon the bread and wine.

For example, if we have experienced pain or hurt in our relationship with our earthly father, we can offer that hurt along with the bread and wine, seeking healing and forgiveness in this relationship. As the priest prays, "By the mystery of this water and wine may we come to share in the divinity of Christ, who humbled himself to share in our humanity," we can unite our brokenness to the brokenness of Christ.

Eucharistic Prayer. At the time of the Eucharistic Prayer, I encourage the people to place their special intentions on the altar, joining them to the perfect and acceptable sacrifice of Christ. In this prayer, Jesus himself takes these intentions and brings them to our Father. When the words of consecration are being prayed by the priest, we can let go of our pain, allowing Jesus to take our pain upon himself on the cross. "He himself bore our sins in his body on the tree, so that we might die to sins and live for righteousness; by his wounds you have been healed" (1 Pt 2:24).

The Our Father. As we pray the Our Father, we can again seek healing in our relationship with God our Father and our human father. We can ask for the grace to be healed of past hurts and try to forgive others. If we find it difficult to forgive, we can ask the Lord for an outpouring of the grace of forgiveness in our lives to help us forgive, or we can ask Jesus to forgive for us until we are able to forgive.

The center of all healing is Jesus Christ. Therefore, as we come to Communion, we should focus our attention on our Lord's unconditional love for us. He totally forgives us. Be open to fully receive him. Ask the Lord to fill you with the healing love of the Holy Spirit.

Holy Communion. Before we receive communion we pray, "Lord, I am not worthy to receive you. Only say the word and I shall be healed." This prayer was taken from the prayer of the centurion in the Gospel of Luke. Jesus responded to this prayer request and healed the centurion's servant. As we say this prayer, we must be confident that Jesus also heals us.

St. Augustine says: "When you receive Holy Communion, you have the Healer Himself." Focus on him. Do not pay attention to who is receiving communion, or what is going on in the church. Take a moment and close your eyes. Imagine Jesus holding you, freeing you of the pain and hurt that you placed upon the altar and united to the sacrifice of Christ. Try to picture the glory of Jesus surrounding you, removing all darkness from you. Or imagine Jesus placing his hand on your heart, healing your emotional pain. Allow him to touch your heart and fill it with his love.

The Concluding Rite. In the final blessing, the concluding rite, the priest, through the power of holy orders, sends you forth to witness, love, serve, and heal one another.

THE POWER OF SACRAMENTALS

Kathy's cousin referred her to me. She was having problems in her house. Things would disappear for a couple of days and then return. Her children would suddenly get sick for no apparent reason. Once two of her children got a sore right ankle (the pain was in exactly the same place) during the night. She did not know where to go for help. She had seen someone who was a spiritualist, and they said that there was a "presence" in the house. Another spiritualist, someone who practiced Chinese divination and magic, tried to get rid of the presence, but it did not leave.

After we talked, I decided to celebrate a Mass in the house. She and her husband invited some close friends over for the Mass. In researching the history of the house, I discovered that an old woman died in the house. Maybe the soul of this woman needed prayer? Maybe these manifestations of illness, injury, and moving objects were her methods of calling for help. In the Mass, we prayed for anyone who died while living in the house, asking that Jesus would heal their lives and take them to heaven if they were suffering in purgatory. I also asked God to send his angels to remove anything that was not of God. After the Mass all seemed calm in their home.

This couple was also experiencing financial difficulties. They ended up losing the home and relocating to an apartment. I wondered, "Is there something I am missing?" I just did not feel right about the work I had done.

A month later I talked to Kathy. She said that her children were getting headaches and upset stomachs. I asked her to bring the children in so I could pray with them. When Kathy and the children came for their appointment, I told her that I was a little confused as to why the children were still getting sick.

She then told me that the Chinese spiritualist had given her these two silver balls. Whenever the children got sick she was to place the balls on their heads and stomachs. When she did this the sickness would leave, but they were getting sick more often. I asked her to let me see the silver balls. I immediately sensed evil when I held them in my hands.

I explained to her that this person was dealing in magic and divination, things prohibited by God. She said he was a Catholic and that is why they trusted him. I responded that one may be Catholic in name, but that Jesus told us that we cannot serve two masters. He was serving the master of darkness and not Jesus. She was able to give up all the things that he had given her. I taught her how to pray using the sacramental of blessed oil. I told her that whenever her children got these headaches or stomach aches, that she was to anoint them with the blessed oil on the forehead, using the sign of the cross. When she anointed she was to pray to God, asking him to heal her children.

The anointing and prayer worked. Each time they would get sick, she would anoint them. The sicknesses became less frequent and gradually stopped. But something else started to happen. They would wake up in the middle of the night, afraid for no apparent reason. The little six-month-old baby would wake up crying at one in the morning, and the other children would wake up as well.

When Kathy realized that she was being led down a path of evil by this man, she told her relatives and friends. She had introduced them to the spiritualist and he was performing divination and magic for them as well. After they heard Kathy's sharing, they stopped seeing him and told other people about him. He gradually lost a lot of business and income. Because of this, the spiritualist started to curse Kathy and her children—that was why they were waking up in the middle of the night.

When Kathy told me that the children were waking up I suggested that she place a blessed candle in their room. When the candle was placed in their room they slept without waking up.

But, you may say, maybe the light from the candle gave them a sense of security, that is why they did not wake up anymore.

But remember that one of these children was only six months old. That baby did not even realize that there was a blessed candle in the room. Kathy even experimented, one day using a regular candle; the next day, a blessed candle. On the day that the regular candle was in the room the baby woke up crying. On the day that the blessed candle was used, the baby slept through the night.

The difference in the candles was that one of them was blessed. A blessed candle is a sacramental. The Catholic Church has instituted sacramentals. These are sacred signs which bear a resemblance to the sacraments. They signify effects, particularly spiritual, which are obtained through the church's intercession. Examples of sacramentals are holy water, blessed salt, blessed oil, blessed candles, vestments, the sign of the cross, rosaries, religious statues, crucifixes, medals of saints, and blessings.

The sacramentals, when used in the proper way, protect us from demonic harassment. We cannot use the sacramentals as superstitions. They are to be used in faith that God will hear our prayer and the church's prayer to protect those who use them. In order to use a sacramental with a proper disposition, we must first be living our faith—going to Mass, receiving the sacraments, and having a daily prayer life.

As Kathy's story illustrates, the sacramentals can be a powerful weapon against the powers of darkness. Using the blessed oil with prayer brought her children physical healing. The blessed candle removed the curse that was continually being placed upon her family.

Sacramental power. We can understand the power of sacramentals through examining their use in normal life (before they are blessed). Water is necessary for life. We wash ourselves with water. Holy water is used to cleanse every place where it is sprinkled from the presence of demonic spirits.

Salt in the ancient world was a precious commodity. Since it was precious, it was an appropriate offering to God. The Israelites were encouraged to "add salt to all your offerings" (Lv 2:13). In fact, salt was used for thirty-five centuries to preserve meats from deterioration. Thus it became a symbol of preservation and spiritual incorruptibility that characterized anyone offering sacrificial worship.

Salt is understood as a sign of a covenantial relationship, to preserve and enrich a relationship (Mk 9:50). Jesus calls his followers the salt of the earth (Mt 5:13). The salt that is saltless, is to be thrown out (Lk 14:34). This refers to Christians who compromise with the world and aren't willing to pay the price of standing up for Christ. Just as salt flavors and preserves food, we are to preserve the good in the world, to help keep it from spoiling and to bring new flavor to life. Being "salty" is not easy, but if a Christian fails in this function, he or she fails to represent Christ in the world.

The first miracle of Elisha is the scriptural basis for the use of blessed salt. Elisha threw salt into already contaminated water and said, "This is what the Lord says: 'I have healed this water. Never again will it cause death or make the land unproductive'" (2 Kgs 2:21).

In the old Roman ritual, blessed salt was added to water to make it blessed water. Blessed salt is used to preserve us from the Evil One and to preserve us in our faith. Used properly, modest amounts of blessed salt may be sprinkled in one's bedroom, on the windowsills, across thresholds, or placed in one's car for safety. A few grains of blessed salt added to drinking water or used in cooking or as food seasoning can bring spiritual and physical benefits. But we must remember to use this sacramental with faith and devotion, not out of superstition. Remember the blind man in John 9. He had faith in Jesus to heal him, not in the mud and spittle that Jesus used.

Oil pressed from olives was also expensive and highly prized in the ancient world. Jacob used oil to anoint the place where God spoke to him (Gn 35:14). Anointing with olive oil showed the high value placed on the anointed object. Olive oil was used in the anointing of wounds (Lk 10:34). Olive oil was also used as a cosmetic. Matthew 6:17 states that when you fast you are to put oil on your head so that no one will know you are fasting.

Blessed oil can be used for healing. When we anoint someone with blessed oil, we make the sign of the cross on his or her forehead or on the injured part of the body and pray that Jesus will heal this person. In Kathy's story, the anointing of her children and the prayer brought healing. Parents can anoint their children each night before they go to bed as a blessing, or use the blessed oil to call for protection if the children are going away from home for vacation or summer camp.

The candle today is symbolic of the lamp in Bible times. The lamp was always kept burning because it was difficult to light. The burning lamp was maintained even in the poorest of homes as a sign that it was lived in or open for business. The extinction of the lamp meant total disaster. King David is called the lamp of Israel (2 Sm 21:17); the survival of his dynasty is a lamp for David (1 Kgs 11:36). The extinction of the lamp signifies the destruction of Judah (Jer 25:10).

In the New Testament, John the Baptist was a lamp, but Jesus is the light (Jn 5:35). A blessed candle symbolizes the light of Jesus Christ, a light that scatters the powers of darkness. In Kathy's story, the blessed candle broke the power of the evil curse. A blessed candle, when properly used, can be a protection against curses and the powers of the Evil One. Here is a blessing of a candle:

Endow these candles Lord by the power of the Holy Cross with a blessing from on high. Let the blessing they receive from the sign of the Holy Cross be so effectual that wherever they are lighted or placed the princes of darkness may depart in trembling from all these places, and flee in fear along with all their legions, never-more there to disturb or molest those who serve you, the almighty God, who lives and reigns forever and ever. Amen.

The sacramentals can be powerful weapons in spiritual warfare. We are to use all the weapons that God has given us because the Enemy is crafty and powerful. But we must remember that we have the most powerful weapon—the name of Jesus. "At the name of Jesus every knee should bow, in heaven and on earth and under the earth, and every tongue confess that Jesus Christ is Lord, to the glory of God the Father" (Phil 2:10-11). In him we have the victory now and forever!

TEN

Victory in Jesus

Jim and Jane had a good relationship. They were not married, yet they loved each other. Since they were not married, they were free to see other people. Jane began to date another man. This affected Jim since he had no desire to date anyone else except Jane. A couple of months passed, and Jane left Jim and went to live with this other man. This relationship was not a healthy relationship. There was physical and emotional abuse, and Jane eventually left the man.

Jim still loved Jane very much, but Jane seemed reticent to speak to him. She realized what she had done and felt very ashamed and guilty. Being a good Christian, Jim prayed fervently for her. Every moment he could spare he would pray for the restoration of the relationship and Jane's healing, even though he did not hear from her.

After a month of prayer, Jim felt that he had to let go of Jane, since she apparently did not want to approach him or was afraid to renew their relationship. Jim was able to forgive Jane for the betrayal that he felt, but he found it difficult to let go.

In prayer he said, "Jesus, I place Jane in your hands, and I let go of her." Daily he prayed, but even though he prayed this, he could not let go. He was afraid that if he really did give her to

Jesus, she might never return to him. His fear was constantly with him. At times he was unable to think clearly. He begged Jesus to remove this fear, but it would not leave.

FREEDOM IN JESUS

One day in prayer Jim sensed that something was not quite right. As he prayed he felt uncomfortable. He was listening to the Lord, seeking a reason why he could not get rid of this fear. Then it dawned on him—there were two sources of his fears: one was normal human fear; the other, demonic. He was being attacked by Satan in a weak area of his life. He immediately renounced the demonic spirit of fear, commanding it in the name of Jesus to go directly to the cross and not to return to him. After that prayer Jim felt a release and he was able to give his human fear to Jesus.

In Jim's life there were two fears. The human fears were a fear of rejection and being alone. The demonic spirit of fear attached itself to these fears and aggravated an emotional disturbance in his life. Only when he commanded the demonic spirit of fear to leave, was he able to let go of the human fear and receive peace.

I believe that many of us live with fear which began in our childhood. The most powerful emotion of childhood is fear, since children want to be safe. They are safe when they have protection from their primary caregivers (hopefully, their parents).

But what happens if they feel rejected by their parents? Then they feel shamed and unloved. The need for love is so great that they will do anything to receive love and get attention. This need for love is an expression of fear. They are so afraid to lose their parents' love that they will do anything.

For example, families have family rules. If a child disobeys one of the rules, they may be punished. This punishment may be a time-out—the child may be told to go to his or her room for a set period of time. Through this discipline, the child learns right and wrong. Some form of discipline is necessary, and gradually the child will learn to obey family rules because of the fear of punishment or lack of love.

For Jim, this fear was ingrained within him. The fear was so deep that a demonic spirit of fear attached itself to him. It would intensify any situation in his life that was fearful. When he realized the root causes (human and demonic) of his fear in his relationship with Jane, he was able to free himself of the fear and live in peace. Now that he is free of the spirit of fear, he can receive a new empowerment of faith and hope in Jesus and accept God's love for him.

HOPE FOR THE BATTLE FATIGUED

We have seen how important it is to have faith, and we know the importance of love for ourselves, God, and others. But there is another virtue that we receive in Baptism. It is the forgotten virtue of hope. When we become exhausted from the spiritual warfare, we experience battle fatigue. Hope assists us when we experience battle fatigue. "We also rejoice in our sufferings, because we know that suffering produces perseverance; perseverance, character; and character, hope. And hope does not disappoint us, because God has poured out his love into our hearts by the Holy Spirit, whom he has given us" (Rom 5:3-5).

Hope is the expectation of a future event. For Christians that means the glory we will share as faithful followers of Jesus Christ. God has given us his Word, and his Word is true. We grow in hope through endurance and the encouragement of the Scriptures (Rom 15:4). As we read and reflect on God's Word, we realize that God does not abandon his people. God has made a covenant with his people, and he will not break it. Even though the Israelites repeatedly sinned in idolatry, God always forgave them when they returned to him and sought forgiveness.

In the Gospel of Matthew, Jesus says, "I am with you always, to the very end of the age" (Mt 28:20). Jesus has promised he will always be with us. He will never abandon us. This is his promise to us, his followers. We have hope in the promises that God has given to us (Acts 26:6-7). And what are God's promises to us?

We hope in the Lord because he delivers us from sin. We cannot deliver ourselves from sin. It is God himself who frees us from our sins (Ps 39:8-9). We rejoice in hope of the glory of God, because through Jesus Christ we have gained access to grace (Rom 5:1-2). We hope in the resurrection of the dead (Acts 23:6) and our union with God forever in heaven. Our faith in God's promises and our knowledge of God's truths rest "on the hope of eternal life, which God, who does not lie, promised before the beginning of time" (Ti 1:2).

God has entered into a sacred covenant with us. He gives us his Word, and he will not break his covenant oath with us. There is a saying—blood is thicker than water. We will stand up for our blood relations because we are united in a unique way with them. But covenant oath with God is thicker than blood.

God desires that we share kinship with him. That is what his covenant with us has done. We share kinship with God, and God will never revoke that kinship. We may revoke our kinship with God through mortal sin—a complete turning away from God. But God will not turn away from us. If we are in mortal sin, all we need to do is go to the sacrament of reconciliation (confession) and seek his forgiveness.

God chose us to be his people. We are purchased for glory through the Blood of Jesus and are being sanctified by the power of the Holy Spirit. God, in his great mercy, has given us a new birth into a living hope through the resurrection of Jesus from the dead (1 Pt 1:2-3). Satan will try to rob us of this gift, but if we stand fast in the Lord he cannot harm us.

The greatest weapon that Satan uses against us is fear. If he can aggravate existing fears, he will drive us into confusion and depression. Remember, our minds are the primary battleground and Satan wants to control and manipulate our minds. That is why it is so important to "take captive every thought to make it obedient to Christ" (2 Cor 10:5).

Hope is the virtue that strengthens us in the spiritual battle, especially when we are weary of the fight. God gave us his covenant so that we could take hold of the hope offered to us and be greatly encouraged. "We have this hope as an anchor for the soul, firm and secure" (Heb 6:19).

The one who hopes is joyful in the Lord (Rom 12:12). The hope-filled Christian waits patiently for the movement of God in his or her life (Rom 8:25). Hope helps us to live a life based on God's commands. We are a people of hope! We know that *Satan cannot destroy us as long as we hope in the Lord.*

FINAL VICTORY

We must always remember that the spiritual battle is Satan against us in union with Jesus. I alone cannot defeat Satan. But I do not have to be afraid because Jesus has already won the victory! In union with Jesus I share in that victory. At times I may not feel victorious, but the reality is that *in Jesus I am victorious.* Jesus and we are the victorious army of God—together we can overcome any difficulty. This is our sure hope.

We must use the weapons that God has given us. We must be vigilant because Satan is a deceiver; he will use anything to divert us away from God. We are to stand fast on the promises that God has given us, realizing he gives us sufficient strength for any trial we have in life (1 Cor 10:13). "The one who is in you is greater than the one who is in the world" (1 Jn 4:4).

To share in the victory of Jesus and defeat Satan in our lives, we must first discern the root causes of our problems. Is it spiritual, emotional, psychological, physical, circumstantial, or physiological in origin? Is Satan aggravating an existing situation? Were we ever involved in the occult?

After this discernment we can come against the Evil One in Jesus. We renounce any occult involvement and use the name of Jesus to cast any demonic oppression out of our lives. We seek healing for our hurts and ask the Holy Spirit to empower us to live a life of holiness, asking God to inflame anew the sacramental graces we have received. We use the gifts of the sacraments, especially Holy Communion and reconciliation, to strengthen us in the daily battle. We read and reflect upon the Word of God and grow in prayer.

We outfit ourselves with the armor of God and seek the assistance of Christians on earth and out heavenly helpers—Mary, the saints, and the angels. We use the sacramentals to protect us from evil interference. God gives us so many gifts to help us in the spiritual battle.

Above all, we must never lose hope. Jesus has won the victory for us; he has promised to never leave us. His precious Blood protects us from harm. No power can separate us from the love of Jesus. Satan cowers when we pray in the power of Jesus' name. We are adopted sons and daughters of God, sharing in the inheritance of Jesus Christ (Rom 8:15-17), an inheritance that can never perish (1 Pt 1:4)!

Who shall separate us from the love of Christ? Shall trouble or hardship or persecution or famine or nakedness or danger or sword? As it is written: "For your sake we face death all day long; we are considered as sheep to be slaughtered." No, in all these things we are more than conquerors through him who loved us. For I am convinced that neither death nor life, neither angels nor demons, neither the present nor the future, nor any powers, neither height nor depth, nor anything else in all creation, will be able to separate us from the love of God that is in Christ Jesus our Lord. **Romans 8:35-39**

In Jesus we have won the victory! May all praise and glory be given to God our Father through Jesus Christ in union with the Holy Spirit!

Appendix

SCRIPTURES ON THE BLOOD OF CHRIST

For the life of a creature is in the blood, and I have given it to you to make atonement for yourselves on the altar; it is the blood that makes atonement for one's life. Leviticus 17:11

But only the high priest entered the inner room, and that only once a year, and never without blood, which he offered for himself and for the sins the people had committed in ignorance....

He [Christ] did not enter by means of the blood of goats and calves; but he entered the Most Holy Place once for all by his own blood, having obtained eternal redemption.... How much more, then, will the blood of Christ, who through the eternal Spirit offered himself unblemished to God, cleanse our consciences from acts that lead to death, so that we may serve the living God! Hebrews 9:7; 12, 14

Then he took the cup, gave thanks and offered it to them, saying "Drink from it, all of you. This is my blood of the covenant, which is poured out for many for the forgiveness of sins." Matthew 26:27-28

God presented him as a sacrifice of atonement, through faith in his blood. He did this to demonstrate his justice, because in his forbearance he had left the sins committed beforehand unpunished—he did it to demonstrate his justice... so as to be just and the one who justifies those who have faith in Jesus. Romans 3:25-26

Since we have now been justified by his blood, how much more shall we be saved from God's wrath through him! For if, when we were God's enemies, we were reconciled to him through the death of his Son, how much more, having been reconciled, shall we be saved through his life! Romans 5:9-10

...In love he predestined us to be adopted as his sons through Jesus Christ....In him we have redemption through his blood, the forgiveness of sins, in accordance with the riches of God's grace that he lavished on us with all wisdom and understanding. Ephesians 1:4-5, 7-8

...at that time you were separate from Christ, excluded from citizenship in Israel and foreigners to the covenants of the promise, without hope and without God in the world. But now in Christ Jesus you who once were far away have been brought near through the blood of Christ. Ephesians 2:12-13

For God was pleased to have all his fullness dwell in him [Christ], and through him to reconcile to himself all things... by making peace through his blood, shed on the cross. Colossians 1:19-20

...to him [Jesus Christ] who loves us and has freed us from our sins by his blood, and has made us to be a kingdom and priests to serve his God and Father—to him be glory and power for ever and ever! Amen. Revelation 1:5-6

...the four living creatures and the twenty-four elders fell down before the lamb. Each one had a harp and they were

holding golden bowls full of incense, which are the prayers
of the saints. And they sang a new song:
   "You are worthy to take the scroll
   and to open its seals,
   because you were slain,
   and with your blood you purchased men for God
   from every tribe and language and people and nation.
   You have made them to be a kingdom and priests to serve
   our God, and they will reign on the earth." Revelation 5:8-10

...These are they who have come out of the great tribula-
tion; they have washed their robes and made them white in
the blood of the lamb. Revelation 7:14

They overcame him [Satan]
by the blood of the Lamb
and by the word of their testimony;
they did not love their lives so much
as to shrink from death. Revelation 12:11

SCRIPTURES FOR THE SPIRITUAL BATTLE

The eternal God is your refuge, and underneath are the everlasting arms. He drives out your enemy before you, saying,
"Destroy him!" Deuteronomy 33:27

The Lord will march out like a mighty man, like a warrior he
will stir up his zeal; with a shout he will raise the battle cry
and will triumph over his enemies. Isaiah 42:13

"... no weapon forged against you will prevail, and you will
refute every tongue that accuses you. This is the heritage of the
servants of the Lord, and this is their vindication from me,"
declares the Lord. Isaiah 54:17

Before they call I will answer; while they are still speaking I will hear. Isaiah 65:24

... nothing is impossible with God.... Blessed is she who has believed that what the Lord has said to her will be accomplished! Luke 1:37, 45

If you remain in me and my words remain in you, ask whatever you wish, and it will be given you. This is to my Father's glory, that you bear much fruit, showing yourselves to be my disciples. John 15:7-8

For [Christ] must reign until he has put all his enemies under his feet. The last enemy to be destroyed is death.... then the saying that is written will come true: "Death has been swallowed up in victory." "Where, O death, is your victory? Where, O death, is your sting?" The sting of death is sin, and the power of sin is the law. But thanks be to God! He gives us the victory through our Lord Jesus Christ.

1 Corinthians 15:25-26; 54-57

Yet he saved them for his name's sake, to make his mighty power known.... He saved them from the hand of the foe; from the hand of the enemy he redeemed them.

Psalm 106:8, 10

In that day they will say, "Surely this is our God; we trusted in him, and he saved us. This is the Lord, we trusted in him; let us rejoice and be glad in his salvation." Isaiah 25:9

...my salvation will last forever, my righteousness will never fail,... my righteousness will last forever, my salvation through all generations. Isaiah 51:6, 8

We all, like sheep, have gone astray, each of us has turned to his own way; and the Lord has laid on him the iniquity of us all.... After the suffering of his soul, he will see the light (of life) and be satisfied; by his knowledge my righteous servant will justify many, and he will hear their iniquities.

Isaiah 53:6, 11

All men will hate you because of me, but he who stands firm to the end will be saved.... Whoever believes and is baptized will be saved, but whoever does not believe will be condemned. Mark 13:13; 16:16

...do not rejoice that the spirits submit to you, but rejoice that your names are written in heaven.... For the Son of Man came to seek and to save what was lost. Luke 10:20; 19:10

For God so loved the world that he gave his one and only son, that whoever believes in him shall not perish but have eternal life. John 3:16

Therefore, there is now no condemnation for those who are in Christ Jesus, because through Christ Jesus the law of the Spirit of life set me free from the law of sin and death.

Romans 8:1-2

...if you confess with your mouth, "Jesus is Lord," and believe in your heart that God raised him from the dead, you will be saved. For it is with your heart that you believe and are justified, and it is with your mouth that you confess and are saved. Romans 10:9-10

For the message of the cross is foolishness to those who are perishing, but to us who are being saved it is the power of God. 1 Corinthians 1:18

Therefore, if anyone is in Christ, he is a new creation; the old has gone, the new has come! 2 Corinthians 5:17

I have been crucified with Christ and I no longer live, but Christ lives in me. The life I live in the body, I live by faith in the Son of God, who loved me and gave himself for me.

Galatians 2:20

Clearly no one is justified before God by the law, because, "The righteous will live by faith.".... Christ redeemed us from the curse of the law by becoming a curse for us, for it is written: "Cursed is everyone who is hung on a tree."

Galatians 3:11, 13

But because of his great love for us, God, who is rich in mercy, made us alive with Christ even when we were dead in transgressions.... And God raised us up with Christ and seated us with him in the heavenly realms in Christ Jesus, in order that in the coming ages he might show the incomparable riches of his grace, expressed in his kindness to us in Christ Jesus. For it is by grace you have been saved, through faith and this not from yourselves, it is the gift of God–not by works, so that no one can boast. Ephesians 2:4-9

If we confess our sins, he is faithful and just and will forgive us our sins and purify us from all unrighteousness. 1 John 1:9

...In his great mercy he has given us new birth into a living hope through the resurrection of Jesus Christ from the dead, and into an inheritance that can never perish, spoil or fade—kept in heaven for you.... 1 Peter 1:3-4

I delight greatly in the Lord; my soul rejoices in my God. For he has clothed me with garments of salvation and arrayed me in a robe of righteousness.... **Isaiah 61:10**

The Lord your God is with you,
he is mighty to save.
He will take great delight in you,
he will quiet you with his love,
he will rejoice over you with singing. **Zephaniah 3:17**

Come to me, all you who are weary and burdened, and I will give you rest. Take my yoke upon you and learn from me, for I am gentle and humble in heart, and you will find rest for your souls. For my yoke is easy and my burden is light.
Matthew 11:28-30

Peace I leave with you; my peace I give you. I do not give to you as the world gives. Do not let your hearts be troubled and do not be afraid. **John 14:27**

If you obey my commands, you will remain in my love, just as I have obeyed my Father's commands and remain in his love. I have told you this so that my joy may be in you and that your joy may be complete. **John 15:10-11**

[God] gives life to the dead and calls things that are not as though they were. Against all hope, Abraham in hope believed and so became the father of many nations, just as it had been said to him.... **Romans 4:17b-18a**

Do not be afraid, little flock, for your Father has been pleased to give you the kingdom. **Luke 12:32**

I have told you these things, so that in me you may have peace. In this world you will have trouble. But take heart! I have overcome the world. John 16:33

For you did not receive a spirit that makes you a slave again to fear, but you received the Spirit of sonship. And by him we cry, "Abba, Father." Romans 8:15

...If God is for us, who can be against us?... For I am convinced that neither death nor life, neither angels nor demons, neither the present nor the future, nor any powers, neither height or depth, nor anything else in all creation, will be able to separate us from the love of God that is in Christ Jesus our Lord. Romans 8:31, 38-39

SCRIPTURES TO BUILD HEALTHY SELF-ESTEEM

I AM:
  A child of God (Rom 8:16).
  Redeemed from the hand of the enemy (Ps 107:2).
  Forgiven (Col 1:13, 14).
  Saved by grace through faith (Eph 2:8).
  Justified (Rom 5:1).
  Sanctified (1 Cor 6:11).
  A new creature (2 Cor 5:17).
  Partaker of his divine nature (2 Pt 1:4).
  Redeemed from the curse of the law (Gal 3:13).
  Delivered from the powers of darkness (Col 1:13).
  Led by the Spirit of God (Rom 8:14).
  A Son or Daughter of God (Rom 8:14).
  Kept in safety wherever I go (Ps 91:11).
  Getting all my needs met by Jesus (Phil 4:19).
  Casting all my cares on Jesus (1 Pt 5:7).

Strong in the Lord and in the power of his might (Eph 6:10).

Doing all things through Christ who strengthens me (Phil 4:13).

An heir of God and joint heirs with Jesus (Rom 8:17).

Heir to the blessings of Abraham (Gal 3:13, 14).

Observing and doing the Lord's commandments (Dt 28:12).

Blessed coming in and going out (Dt 28:6).

An inheritor of eternal life (1 Jn 5:11-12).

Blessed with all spiritual blessings (Eph 1:3).

Exercising my authority over the Enemy (Lk 10:19).

More than a conqueror (Rom 8:37).

An overcomer by the Blood of the Lamb and the Word of my testimony (Rv 12:11).

Notes

ONE
Faith

1. Karl Rahner, *Encyclopedia of Theology: The Concise Sacramentum Mundi* (New York: Seabury, 1984), 508.
2. For an excellent explanation of the New Age Movement, I recommend *Catholics and the New Age*, Fr. Mitch Pacwa (Ann Arbor, Mich.: Servant, 1992).
3. Elliot Miller, *A Crash Course on the New Age Movement* (Grand Rapids, Mich.: Baker, 1989), 14-15.
4. Fr. Jeffrey Steffon, *Satanism: Is It Real?* (Ann Arbor, Mich.: Servant, 1992), 93.
5. *Humanist Manifesto II*, as cited in Ralph Martin, *A Crisis of Truth* (Ann Arbor, Mich.: Servant, 1982), 100-101.
6. Martin, 102.
7. Benedict Groeschel, *Spiritual Passages: The Psychology of Spiritual Development* (New York: Crossroad, 1983), 96.
8. Rahner, 496.

TWO
Is Satan Real?

1. An exorcism is performed when it is believed that a person is possessed by Satan. There are strict rules to be followed. In order for a person to receive an exorcism, they must first go through a series of psychological examinations. An exorcism is only performed with the bishop's permission after all examinations have been completed.
2. Rahner, 341.
3. Rahner, 342.
4. John McKenzie, ed. *Dictionary of the Bible* (New York: Macmillan, 1965); *Biblical Commentary* (Englewood Cliffs, NJ: Prentice Hall, 1990), 71-72.
5. Charles Harris, C.S.C., *Resist the Devil* (South Bend, Ind,: Greenlawn Press, 1988), 4.

6. Justin Martyr, "Second Apology" VI, translated by Thomas B. Falls in *The Fathers of the Church* (New York: Christian Heritage, 1948), 125-126.

7. Iraneus, "Against Heretics," II. 32, 4; translated by Rev. Alexander Roberts, et. al. in *Ante-Nicene Christian Library*, Vol. 5 (Edinburgh: T & T Clark, 1884), 245-246.

8. Ignatius of Antioch, "Letter to the Ephesians," 13, *The Fathers of the Church*, 92.

9. E.H. Gifford, "St. Cyril of Jerusalem and St. Gregory Nanzienzen," in *Library of Nicene and Post-Nicene Fathers*, Second Series, Vol. 7 (New York: Christian Literature Company, 1984), xix.

10. Origen, "Against Celus," *Ante-Nicene Christian Library*, Vol. 10, 402.

11. *The Christian Faith in the Doctrinal Documents of the Catholic Church*, as cited in Harris, *Resist the Devil*, 101.

12. Walter Abbott, ed. *The Documents of Vatican II*, "The Dogmatic Constitution on the Church" (New York: Corpus Books, 1966), paragraph 16.

13. Abbott, *Vatican II*, "Dogmatic Constitution on the Sacred Liturgy," no. 6.

14. Abbott, *Vatican II*, "Decree on the Church's Missionary Activity," no. 3.

15. Abbott, *Vatican II*, "Decree on the Church's Missionary Activity," no. 9.

16. Abbott, *Vatican II*, "Pastoral Constitution on the Church in the Modern World," no. 2.

17. *L'Osservatore Romano*, English language ed. (November 23, 1972), 3.

18. *The Roman Ritual: Rite of Baptism for Children* (New York: Catholic Book, 1970-1977), 33.

19. *The Rites of the Catholic Church* (New York: Pueblo Publishing, 1976), 75.

20. Austin Flannery, *Vatican Council II: More Postconciliar Documents*, as cited in Harris, *Resist the Devil*, 105-106.

THREE

Satan: His Nature and Activity in the World

1. Harris, 4.

FOUR

Redemption through Jesus Christ

1. Andrew Murray, *The Power of the Blood of Jesus* (Grand Rapids, Mich.: Zondervan, 1987), 27.

2. St. Fulgentius of Ruspe, *A Treatise on Faith Addressed to Peter* as cited in *The Liturgy of the Hours* Office of Readings, Friday, Fifth Week of Lent (New York: Catholic Book, 383-384.

3. Murray, 41.

4. *The Exultet*, as cited in *The Roman Missal, The Sacramentary* (New York: Catholic Book, 1970-1977), 182-186.

FIVE
Our Heavenly Helpers

1. Paul O'Sullivan, O.P. *All About the Angels* (Rockford, Ill.: Tan, 1990), 19-21.
2. Pope John Paul II. *A Catechesis of the Angels* (July, 1986), as cited in *Angel of God My Guardian Dear* (Barto, Pa.: National Center for Padre Pio, 1986), 32.
3. Pope John Paul II, *A Catechesis*, 33.
4. Pope John Paul II, *A Catechesis*, 43.
5. Pope John Paul II, *A Catechesis*, 48.
6. Pope John Paul II, *A Catechesis*, 48.
7. Pope John Paul II, *A Catechesis*, 49.
8. Pope John Paul II, *A Catechesis*, 48.
9. Abbot, *Vatican II*, "Dogmatic Constitution on the Church," paragraph 66.
10. Fr. Rene Laurentin, *The Hail Mary, Its Meaning and Its Origin* (Milford, Ohio: Faith Publishing, 1991), 51-52.
11. George M. Montague, *Our Father, Our Mother, Mary and the Faces of God* (Steubenville, Ohio: Franciscan University Press), 139.
12. George Kosicki, *Spiritual Warfare: The Attack Against the Woman* (Milford, Ohio: Faith Publishing, 1990), 11.
13. Kosicki, 14.
14. Kosicki, 14.
15. National Conference of Catholic Bishops, *Behold Your Mother* (Washington, DC: United States Catholic Conference, 1973), 82.
16. Karl Keating, *Catholicism and Fundamentalism* (San Francisco: Ignatius Press, 1988), 269.
17. Keating, 270.
18. Keating, 278.
19. *Behold Your Mother*, 93.
20. Keating, 261.
21. Keating, 263.

SIX
The Battle Within

1. Thomas White, *The Believer's Guide to Spiritual Warfare*, (Ann Arbor, Mich.: Servant, 1990), 21.
2. Gershen Kaufman, *Shame, the Power of Caring* (Rochester, Vt.: Schenkman Books, 1985), 69.
3. John Bradshaw, *Healing the Shame that Binds You* (Deerfield, Fla.: Health Communications, 1988), 18.
4. Kaufman, 73.
5. Kaufman, 90-91.
6. Kaufman, 12.
7. Kaufman, 124.
8. White, 54.
9. Groeschel, 94-95.

SEVEN
The Battle around Us

1. White, 71.
2. White, 77.
3. John McKenzie, *Dictionary of the Bible* (New York: Macmillan, 1965), 943.
4. McKenzie, 943.

EIGHT
How Demonic Oppression Works

1. Charles Kraft, *Defeating Dark Angels* (Ann Arbor, Mich.: Servant, 1992), 95.
2. Mark Johnson, *Spiritual Warfare for the Wounded* (Ann Arbor, Mich.: Servant, 1992), 38.
3. David Stoop, *Forgiving Our Parents, Forgiving Ourselves* (Ann Arbor, Mich.: Servant, 1991), 75.
4. Bradshaw, 17-18.
5. Stoop, 107.
6. White, 88.
7. White, 89-90.
8. White, 91.
9. A sermon by Baldwin of Canterbury, Bishop, as cited in *The Liturgy of the Hours*, Office of Readings, Friday, Ninth Week in Ordinary Time (New York: Catholic Book, 1976).

NINE
Our Weapons for Battle

1. Steffon, *Satanism*, 43.
2. Steffon, 65.
3. Steffon, 73.
4. Domenico Marcucci, *Through the Rosary with Fra Angelico* (New York: Alba House, 1989), 5.
5. Marcucci, 5.
6. *O Angel of God my Guardian Dear*, 24.
7. Eddie Ensley, *Sounds of Wonder* (New York: Paulist Press, 1977), 3.
8. Ensley, 3, 14.

Bibliography

Abbott, Walter M., ed. *The Documents of Vatican II*. New York: Corpus Books, 1966.

Ante-Nicene Christian Library. Edinburgh, London: T & T Clark, 1884.

Bradshaw, John. *Healing the Shame that Binds You*. Deerfield Beach, Fla.: Health Communications, 1988.

Daniélou, Jean. trans. by David Heimann, *The Angels and Their Mission*. Westminister, MD: Christian Classics, 1957.

DeGrandis, Fr. Robert, S.S.J. *Healing through the Mass*. Mineola, New York: Resurrection Press, 1992.

DeGrandis, Fr. Robert, S.S.J. *Intergenerational Healing*. 1989.

Ensley, Eddie. *Sounds of Wonder*. New York: Paulist Press, 1977.

The Enthronement and Family Consecration to the Sacred Heart. Paco, Manila: Apostleship of Prayer, 1987.

Falls, Thomas B. trans. *The Fathers of the Church*. New York: Christian Heritage, 1948.

Flannery, Austin, ed. *Les Formes de la Superstitution* in *Vatican Council II: More Post-Conciliar Documents*. Northport: Costello, 1982.

Fox, Fr. Robert. *The World and Work of the Holy Angels*. Alexandria, SD: Fatima Family Apostolate, 1991.

Green, Michael. *Exposing the Prince of Darkness*. Ann Arbor, Mich.: Servant, 1981.

Groeschel, Benedict. *Spiritual Passages: The Psychology of Spiritual Development*. New York: Crossroad, 1983.

Harris, Charles, C.S.C. *Resist the Devil*. South Bend, IN: Greenlawn Press, 1988.

Johnson, Mark. *Spiritual Warfare for the Wounded*. Ann Arbor, Mich.: Servant, 1992.

Kaufman, Gershen. *Shame: The Power of Caring*. Rochester, Vt.: Shenkman Books, 1985.

Keating, Karl. *Catholicism and Fundamentalism*. San Francisco: Ignatius Press, 1988.

Kelsey, Morton. *Discernment: A Study in Ecstasy and Evil.* New York: Paulist, 1978.

Kosicki, Rev. George. *Spiritual Warfare: The Attack against the Woman.* Milford, Ohio: Faith, 1990.

Kraft, Charles. *Defeating Dark Angels.* Ann Arbor, Mich.: Servant, 1992.

Laurentin, Fr. Rene. *The Hail Mary.* Milford, Ohio: Faith Publishing, 1991.

L'Observatore Romano. English language ed. (November 23, 1972).

The Liturgy of the Hours According to the Roman Rite. New York: Catholic Book, 1976.

Library of Nicene and Post-Nicene Fathers, Second Series. New York: Christian Literature, 1984.

Marcucci, Domenico. *Through the Rosary with Fra Angelico.* New York: Alba House, 1989.

McKenzie, John. *Dictionary of the Bible.* New York: Macmillan, 1965.

Martin, Ralph. *A Crisis of Truth.* Ann Arbor, Mich.: Servant, 1982.

Miller, Elliot. *A Crash Course on the New Age Movement.* Grand Rapids, Mich.: Baker, 1989.

Montague, George. *Our Father, Our Mother, Mary and the Faces of God.* Steubenville, Ohio: Franciscan University Press, 1990.

Montrose, Rev. Donald. *Spiritual Warfare: The Occult Has Demonic Influence.* Washington, N.J.: AMI Press, 1992.

Murray, Andrew. *The Power of the Blood of Jesus.* Grand Rapids, Mich.: Zondervan, 1987.

National Conference of Catholic Bishops. *Behold Your Mother.* Washington, D.C.: United States Catholic Conference, 1973.

The New Jerome Biblical Commentary. Englewood, N.J.: Prentice Hall, 1990.

O Angel of God My Guardian Dear. Barto, Pa.: National Center for Padre Pio, 1986.

O'Sullivan, Fr. Paul. *All About the Angels.* Rockford, Ill.: Tan, 1990.

Pacwa, Mitch. *Catholics and the New Age.* Ann Arbor, Mich.: Servant, 1992.

Paine, Rev. Randall. *The Angels Are Waiting.* St. Paul, Minn.: Leaflet Missal, 1988.

Parente, Fr. Pascal. *Beyond Space.* Rockford, IL: Tan, 1973.

Pope John Paul II. *Mother of the Redeemer.* Boston, Mass.: Daughters of St. Paul, 1987.

Rahner, Karl. ed. *Encyclopedia of Theology: The Concise Sacramentum Mundi.* New York: Seabury Press, 1984.

The Rites of the Catholic Church. New York: Pueblo Publishing, 1976.

The Roman Ritual: Rite of Baptism for Children. New York: Catholic Book, 1970-1977.

Sherrer, Quin and Garlock, Ruthanne. *The Spiritual Warrior's Prayer Guide.* Ann Arbor, Mich.: Servant, 1992.

Steffon, Fr. Jeffrey. *Satanism: Is It Real?* Ann Arbor, Mich.: Servant, 1992.

Stoop, David. *Forgiving Our Parents, Forgiving Ourselves.* Ann Arbor, Mich.: Servant, 1991.

White, Thomas. *The Believer's Guide to Spiritual Warfare.* Ann Arbor, Mich.: Servant, 1990.

Another Book by the Author
of Interest to Charis Book Readers

Satanism
Is It Real?

Fr. Jeffrey J. Steffon

Law enforcement officials nationwide are increasingly uncovering cases of satanic ritual abuse, some even involving small children. Teenagers are being lured into satanism by drugs, sex, and heavy-metal rock bands. This is the ugly face of satanism today. What can you do to meet this threat, especially if you are a parent who is justifiably concerned for the safety and well-being of your children?

Providing perspective and practical help, Fr. Jeffrey Steffon presents Catholicism's consistent teaching on Satan and the occult, explores present-day satanism and its roots, and shows how occult and New Age practices can become doorways to satanism. He also identifies telltale signs of ritual abuse in small children, provides expert advice on keeping teenagers out of satanism, and explains how to use the church's centuries-old deliverance prayer in combating demons.

Satanism: Is It Real? is an essential guide for parents, pastors, and youth counselors, to help them meet this growing menace both at home and in the parish. *$8.99*